English. The book is a complete anatomy of a major educational enterprise, and as such it will stand for years as the most authoritative description of college English. When college English educators want to know how many departments have which teaching loads, they will find the answer here. If they want to compare the size of their classes with the national average, they will be able to do so. If they plan to start an honors program, they will find a succinct account of how such programs are conducted. A "Checklist for Departments," forty practical questions which departments may put to themselves as they reexamine their programs, is included. By running through this checklist and by comparing their practices with those described in the main part of the book, English departments can make a probing analysis of their own operations.

Every English department, every college and university which hopes to avoid provincialism, duplication of effort, and costly mistakes as it reviews and revises its curriculum for undergraduates will welcome this rich compendium of information and suggestions.

THE AUTHOR

THOMAS W. WILCOX is professor of English and director of the freshman English program at the University of Connecticut.

The Anatomy
of
College English

Thomas W. Wilcox

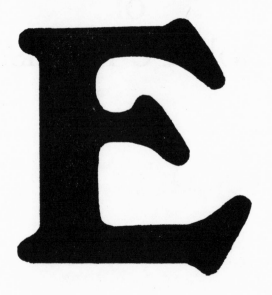

THE
ANATOMY
OF
COLLEGE
ENGLISH

Jossey-Bass Publishers
San Francisco • Washington • London • 1973

THE ANATOMY OF COLLEGE ENGLISH
by Thomas W. Wilcox

Copyright © 1973 by Jossey-Bass, Inc., Publishers
615 Montgomery Street
San Francisco, California 94111

Published and copyrighted in Great Britain by
Jossey-Bass, Ltd., Publishers
3 Henrietta Street
London WC2E 8LU

Library of Congress Catalogue Card Number LC 72-11970

International Standard Book Number ISBN 0-87589-163-2

Manufactured in the United States of America

JACKET DESIGN BY WILLI BAUM

FIRST EDITION

Code 7306

The
Jossey-Bass Series
in Higher Education

For THEODORE BAIRD
whose teaching changed me

Preface

The Anatomy of College English offers teachers, departmental officers, administrators, and all others who are concerned with higher education a comprehensive description and analysis of undergraduate English as it is taught in four-year colleges and universities throughout the United States. The purpose of this study is to define and appraise a major academic institution—one that has been discussed (and attacked) for decades but that has never before been surveyed as a whole. My book is divided into ten chapters and an appendix. I begin with a description of the English department itself: its structure, size, and governance. In these opening chapters I also discuss such matters as staffing, tenure and promotion, evaluating teaching, and work loads. I then turn to the department's general responsibility to the academic community. I review its adjunct and service programs—including that monster, freshman English—and the instruction it provides for nonspecialists. Next I proceed to the major in English and describe programs for those who elect to concentrate in the field. Finally I comment on the general health of undergraduate English and on some of the urgent problems departments confront today. In the appendix I offer a checklist or series of questions most departments will want to answer as they review their own programs for undergraduates.

This book is based on an extensive survey I conducted in 1967–68 and on three years of subsequent investigation. My original study, which bore the grand (but accurate) title "The National Survey of Undergraduate Programs in English," was inaugurated by the National Council of Teachers of English and funded by the United States Office of Education. Guided by such experts in surveying techniques as William C. Budd of Western Washington State College, Jerold Heiss of the University of Connecticut, and the Survey Research Center of the University of Michigan, I first set about to determine just what my survey should determine—that is, to define its scope and to decide what questions I should pose, what information I should seek. During this preliminary stage I visited some fifteen departments of English in colleges and universities of different kinds in different parts of the country to ask their members what they would look for if they were conducting such an investigation. I also met several times with an advisory committee, whose chairman was Glenn Leggett of Grinnell College. From these deliberations and consultations a preliminary agenda for the survey emerged.

For purely practical reasons, we decided to limit our investigation to colleges and universities that offer four-year programs in English. We were well aware of the important role the junior and community colleges play in the education of undergraduates and of the close relationship between their programs and those of the four-year institutions. But the compass of our survey had to be of manageable size, and for this reason alone the two-year colleges were excluded from its purview.

I began the survey proper by proceeding directly into the field, conducting on-the-spot interviews at sixty-three colleges and universities in an effort to define recurrent patterns in undergraduate programs and to identify the major concerns of college English departments. Almost every department I visited suffered my lengthy interrogations with great good will, and by the end of the ten months I devoted to these interviews I found I had acquired an enormous fund of professional lore. Most of the illustrative examples I cite in

The Anatomy of College English were collected during that phase of my study.

By collating various lists and by writing directly to hundreds of departments, I ascertained that exactly 1320 colleges and universities were offering four-year programs in English. (By 1972, that number had risen to 1526, according to the MLA.) This was the universe I was to survey comprehensively; and, since I clearly could not visit all the schools or even an adequate sample of the whole, I would have to conduct my survey by mail. Accordingly, I set about to devise, with the help of the advisory committee, an instrument that would elicit complete and reliable information on national practices in those matters which my interviews had revealed to be of greatest importance to departments of English. My questionnaire (which ran to thirty-nine pages in its final form) was pretested on a number of departments and mailed to a scientifically selected random sample of 300 departments. The response was astonishing: 284 departments, or 94.6 percent of the sample, returned the questionnaire; thus, the information I gleaned from their replies was bound to be highly accurate and reliable. My assistants and I analyzed, coded, and tabulated those replies; and I then undertook the considerable task of composing all I had learned into a comprehensive final report.

That document was filed with the Bureau of Research, Office of Education, in the spring of 1970. It contains a complete account of how the survey was conducted (including a copy of the questionnaire), ninety-one tables, and footnotes for all quotations. Copies of my final report may be obtained from ERIC Document Reproduction Service, LEASCO Information Products, Inc., P.O. Box Drawer 0, Bethesda, Maryland 20014. The accession number is ED 044 422, and the title is *A Comprehensive Survey of Undergraduate Programs in English in the United States.*

Since completing my report I have continued my English-watching by corresponding with many members of the profession, attending numerous meetings and conferences, and visiting another fourteen campuses. Certain events—particularly the sudden reversal of the job market and the demonstrations of student discontent—threatened to render some of my original findings obsolete; English, like many other academic institutions, seemed due for a drastic change. Now it does not appear that those events had an immediate and profound effect on undergraduate programs; certainly they did not prompt the widespread revision of curriculums some thought appropriate. Ominous new trends are now discernible, however, trends which may be seen as delayed consequences of the upheavals of 1969 and 1970. The public's respect and affection for its institutions of higher education have diminished just at a time when the cost of such education has greatly increased, and the same economic influences which have imposed austerity on the colleges and universities have made it difficult for their graduates to find jobs. Frightened by their bleak prospects, students are reluctant to indulge in such "luxuries" as courses in the humanities. Enrollments in English began to decline in 1972 as students sought economic security by acquiring practical, vocational training. I have referred to these trends at appropriate points throughout *The Anatomy of College English* and have speculated on how they might affect the statistics I compiled at an earlier, happier date. Although I have used the present tense in presenting most of my original findings, I have been careful to switch to the past whenever it appeared that my statistics might not be accurate now.

Here, then, are the facts about undergraduate English. Some will construe this evidence differently, will reach conclusions different from those I draw in my final chapter (and imply by some of the loaded questions I include in my Checklist for Departments). I will be pleased if they do, especially if they make their conclusions known. I shall be disappointed if my assertions do not provoke debate among those who share my concern for the welfare of undergraduate English.

I should like to express my gratitude to the many persons who helped me conduct the survey and prepare *The Anatomy of College English*. The members of the advisory committee—Robert Daniel, Leonard F. Dean, John H. Fisher, Gerhart Friedrich, Bruce Harkness, Glenn Leggett, James R. Squire, and William S. Ward—provided invaluable counsel and encouragement. Officers of the National Council of Teachers of English—especially Robert F. Hogan and Mary T. Gerhart—and of the Modern Language Association—especially Michael F. Shugrue, the English secretary—were unfailingly patient and cooperative. Shugrue was enormously helpful during all phases of this project. My technical advisors, William C. Budd and Jerold Heiss, prevented me from committing numerous errors. Arthur Applebee generously provided editorial assistance as I was preparing my final report. The following members of the survey staff labored to compile its findings: Margery Banks, Barbara Churchill, Erben Cook III, Patricia W. Cook, Dorothy Peckham, David Thomen, and William Thomen. And my colleagues at the University of Connecticut—especially Irving Cummings, Thomas J. Roberts, and Roger Wilkenfeld—sustained me with excellent shoptalk and suggestions.

Parts of this book have appeared in the *ADE Bulletin*, published by the Association of Departments of English, and in *College English*, published by the National Council of Teachers of English. I am grateful to those organizations for permission to reprint.

My special thanks go to Darleen B. Wilcox, who suffered much and contributed much.

Storrs, Connecticut   THOMAS W. WILCOX
January 1973

Contents

The Anatomy
of
College English

ONE

The Department of English: Structure and Operations

At 81.1 percent of all four-year colleges and universities, the department of English is a separate organizational entity, all of whose members teach English or closely related subjects. At the remaining 18.9 percent, those who teach English join teachers of other disciplines—the foreign languages, history, or philosophy, for example—in consolidated departments. Where such amalgamations occur, they can be attributed to the smallness of the school (42.3 percent of all cases), administrative convenience (19.2 percent), historical accident (7.7), common programs (3.8), or other special circumstances (15.4). The resulting hybrid is usually called either the Department of Humanities or the Department of Language and Literature, but other terms—

such as the Department of Language Arts and the Department of Communications—are also used. The undergraduate programs in English offered by amalgamated departments do *not* differ significantly from those offered by the more common integral departments of English: the number of interdisciplinary courses is no greater, nor are there more courses in comparative literature. In short, where English is yoked with other disciplines, the union is usually a marriage of convenience rather than a consequence of some radical revision of the conventional institutional structure.

Some institutions—10.8 percent, to be exact—have more than one department of English or staff of English teachers. Most of them are universities at which certain duties which normally devolve to the department of English have been delegated to other departments or at which technical schools offer their own programs in English. Thus, English as a second language is taught by members of the Department of Foreign Languages at Lewis and Clark University; and at both the University of Colorado and the University of Virginia, the College of Engineering maintains a staff of specially qualified instructors who conduct courses in English appropriate to the needs and interests of technologically minded students. At the University of Minnesota, English is taught by four separate faculty groups: the Division of Literature, Speech, and Writing (General College); the Program in Communication; the Department of Rhetoric (schools of agriculture, forestry, and home economics); and the Department of English. Such Balkanization is rare, however; on most campuses the English department alone teaches English as such, and it remains a discrete component of the institutional structure.

Size

At over two thirds (67.6 percent) of all four-year colleges and universities, English is the largest department in number of full-time members; at another 4.8 percent, it is tied for largest. Its nearest competitors for this distinction are education (which is larger than English on 8.1 percent of all campuses), music (5.5 percent), religion (4.8), physical science (4.4), social studies (4), and foreign languages (4). But the relative size of the English department cannot be ascribed to popularity alone: very few other departments are obliged, as English is, to staff freshman and soph-omore courses that are required of most students or that satisfy group requirements. The service obligations of the English depart-ment and its participation in general programs for lower-division students may account for as much as half its size. (Freshman English alone consumes 40 percent of its total teaching effort.) If it were not entrusted with a large captive audience, the English department's size might equal those of such departments as psy-chology and history.

In 1967, college English departments ranged in size from one to about one hundred full-time members: the largest I found was that at the Champaign-Urbana campus of the University of Illinois (99 5/6 full-time equivalents). Exactly half of all English depart-ments in four-year colleges and universities had fewer than ten members, 64.3 percent had fewer than fifteen, and 15 percent had more than thirty members. At that time, 1320 institutions offered four-year programs in English, and they employed approximately 21,000 full-time teachers. Of these, 21.1 percent taught at small colleges, 13 percent at medium-sized colleges and universities, and 65.8 percent at large universities (I classified institutions as "small" if they had fewer than 1500 undergraduates, "medium-sized" if they had 1501 to 2500, and "large" if they had over 2500); 63.2 percent of these teachers were at public schools, 24.1 percent at private, and 12.6 percent at sectarian. The large public universities employed 55.6 percent of all college English teachers. The total number may have diminished slightly in the ensuing years as financial pressures have forced the colleges and universities to increase teaching loads and to eliminate teaching positions.

Some sense of the English department's size in relation to the institution's total undergraduate enrollment is conveyed by the following statistics: colleges with under 300 students employed an average of 2.1 teachers of English; with 300–600 students, 4.6 teachers; 601–1000, 6.3; 1001–1500, 8.7; 1501–2000, 12.6; 2001–2500, 17.2; 2501–3000, 22.6; 3001–8000, 27.9; 8001–12,000, 41.4; and over 12,000, 63.3. These figures may enable us to identify gross anomalies—to say, for example, that an English department of twenty in a school that has 3500 undergraduates is probably understaffed; but they do not tell us precisely how large a given department should be. And, indeed, no simple, practical formula for determining the proper size of a department can be devised. So much depends on such variables as the department's normal teaching load, the class size it permits, the demand for its major, and the extent of its commitment to graduate education that it would be difficult and probably futile to prescribe an optimum ratio of English teachers to undergraduate enrollments for all institutions. Very few departments estimate their needs and regulate their size by applying such a formula; most add or eliminate positions more or less haphazardly as student demand increases or decreases and as funds are supplied or denied by the administration. Even such burgeoning departments as that at the State University of New York at Buffalo, which expected to expand from 63 members in 1967 to 140 in 1970 (but settled for 73 in 1972), do not proceed according to a carefully planned schedule of growth; instead, they must annually appeal to their deans and provosts for their share of what money is available. Only 7 percent of all departments had fixed tables of organization or specified quotas for each rank in 1967; and although there is now much talk of "master plans," "long-range projections," and the infamous "Program Planning and Budget System," it is still true that the size of the English department is often conditioned by such extra-academic influences as the disposition of the governor and the state of the general economy. In short, the size of the department of English is usually determined by local circumstances and contingencies; it is seldom the product of systematic calculation.

Internal Structure

All English departments, except a very few in certain sectarian institutions, have hierarchical structures. Not all identify their members by rank: Bennington College, for example, makes no distinctions of rank, and all the teachers who compose the Department of Language and Literature are known as "instructors" or "members of the faculty." But even at such egalitarian institutions (less than 1 percent of all those offering four-year programs in English), teachers are variously rewarded for their services, and thus an economic, if not a titular, hierarchy obtains.

At over 98 percent of colleges and universities, the conventional titles *professor, associate professor, assistant professor,* and *instructor* are used to designate the principal ranks. The distribution of English teachers among these ranks varies greatly among departments, but the average percentage at each rank is as follows: professor: 20.8; associate professor: 18.6; assistant professor: 33.9; instructor: 26.5. Many college administrators and some department chairmen suppose that the hierarchical structure of a department should be pyramidal, that a process of natural selection should allow only a small percentage of teachers to reach the top. These statistics reveal, however, that this ideal configuration is seldom achieved. Just as it is difficult to regulate the growth of a department—to assure, that is, that its size will always conform to some careful calculation of its needs—so it is difficult to prevent disproportionate distribution of its members among the ranks. Two kinds of disproportion, top-heaviness and bottom-heaviness, are most common among departments of English. The former occurs when over half the members are professors or associate professors. The University of Chicago, for example, had twenty-two professors of English and ten associate professors but only fourteen assistant professors and four instructors in 1967. Several other departments— those at Yale, Haverford, DePauw, Grinnell, Kenyon, Beloit, Mills, and Pomona, to name but a few—were similarly top-heavy. Many of these are relatively small departments; indeed, top-heaviness seems to be most common in small colleges, probably because such institutions are especially susceptible to the causes of such imbalance. The first of these causes is simply that teachers of English often find their work and the circumstances under which they teach reasonably congenial (or they find, after their first ten years as college teachers, that their services are not in great demand elsewhere), and so they devote their professional careers to rising in the hierarchies of the departments to which they are committed. Because their performances are unimpeachable, they cannot—and, in most cases, should not—be denied promotion. Thus, they rise to the top; and if there are many of the same generation in one department, that department becomes top-heavy. This is precisely what has happened at several excellent small colleges, whose English teachers have no desire to leave and every right to expect promotion.

It also happens, and with increasing frequency, that promotions are awarded in lieu of financial rewards, with the result that departments become overloaded and underpaid. This practice, which inevitably devalues the upper ranks, is common among impecunious institutions, of which there now are many. Lacking funds to provide regular increments, administrators resort to bestowing early promotions without corresponding raises in salary. Sooner or later this illusory procedure results in a glut at the top.

During the expansion of the 1960s and before the retrenchment of the early 1970s the concept and significance of the professorship, the associate professorship, and the assistant professorship were liberalized or redefined at many institutions; as a result, department members qualified more readily than ever before for promotion to the upper ranks. As one department chairman said in an interview, "In the past you had to publish a book to be promoted to associate; now you just have to stay around long enough." This willingness to waive or to relax requirements was attributable largely to the shortage of competent teachers and to the competition for well-qualified personnel which then prevailed; in a sellers' market, employers could not afford to insist on standards and policies that might seem arbitrary and oppressive to those whose services they wished to retain. But this redefinition of rank was also a consequence of the general growth of higher education: with students demanding more instruction, departments grew and found more occasions for rewarding good service with promotion. Thus, the whole hierarchy of academic rank was translated upward, so that what was formerly meant by "assistant professor" was now designated by "associate professor," and so on. A new story or penthouse was then added to the academic structure with the creation of a kind of super-rank, variously titled "distinguished professor" or "university professor," with the establishing of several highly endowed chairs for senior professors, and with the extension of salary scales at some state universities to include such top categories as "maximum plus one." This trend toward top-heaviness has now been arrested or reversed as beleaguered administrators on many campuses have reinstituted older, stricter criteria for promotion and have left their super-ranks unfilled.

Top-heaviness impairs a department and its program only when it causes clogging and stagnation. Many good departments of

English have more professors than assistant professors, and this imbalance seems to have little adverse effect on their programs for undergraduates. If courses are not rotated however, if junior members are prevented from exercising their fresh competence and manifesting their enthusiasm, and if their view from the bottom of the hierarchy is bleak or blocked, top-heaviness may be ruinous to morale and may seriously affect the quality of instruction offered to students.

Some departments suffer from extreme bottom-heaviness. At one state university in the Midwest, for example, the English department had eighty-three full-time teachers in 1967, and 77 percent of them were below the rank of associate professor. (This department also employed twenty-four teaching assistants.) At another large public institution the 41 full-time members were "assisted" by 157 part-time teachers! Such imbalance could mean only that these departments had become overdependent on the inexpensive services of inexperienced teachers. A majority of their undergraduate courses (including over 90 percent of their freshman programs) were taught by junior members, temporary appointees, and apprentice teachers. To redress the balance and to redistribute teaching assignments among department members at all ranks would have required expending large sums of money, which these institutions were unable even then to provide. Meanwhile, the effects of such grotesque imbalance on the morale of the department and on the quality of the instruction it offers are obvious.

The Rank of Instructor

Several bottom-heavy departments employed whole platoons of instructors, but in 1967 it seemed that rank was about to disappear. Both the University of California and Indiana University had abolished it, appointing only at the rank of assistant professor and above. That practice was not yet widespread—81 percent of all departments retained the rank of instructor in 1967, and the number may have increased in the lean years since; but many departments indicated their desire to follow the examples of these large, prestigious institutions. The trend toward eliminating the lowest rank coincided with (and may have been causally related to) a trend toward eliminating, reducing, or enriching that portion of the undergraduate program which is so often delegated to junior staff members: freshman English. If the courses that departments offered to freshmen were redesigned to make them more substantial and more demanding, it may have been because conventional programs were deemed unsuited, not only to today's entering students but also to today's beginning teachers, many of whom had skipped the rank of instructor and, they presumed, the menial duties it has traditionally entailed.

Incidence of Ph.D.s

The rank of instructor has commonly been reserved for those teachers who have not acquired the doctorate; indeed, at many institutions promotion to assistant professor is granted automatically when the doctorate is acquired. It might be supposed, therefore, that the percentage of Ph.D.s among professors of English is high. In fact, it is not. The average percentage of department members above the rank of instructor who have the doctorate is 52. If we include instructors, that percentage drops to 37.6. The incidence of Ph.D.s among English teachers above the rank of instructor is highest in large public institutions that offer graduate programs in English, and it is appreciably higher among departments in the Western and North Atlantic regions than among departments in the South. Evaluation of English departments and education in English would be greatly simplified if this single figure, the percentage of department members holding the Ph.D., were an infallible index of quality. Unfortunately, it is not. Some departments with few Ph.D.s among their members still provide good instruction in English; others have a high percentage of Ph.D.s but offer nothing but stale and ineffective programs for undergraduates. Too often today the title "Doctor of Philosophy" designates little more than the completion of a course of graduate studies, and that achievement does not ensure good teaching. For this reason and others it is quite fallacious to rate departments and their programs solely according to the number and kinds of degrees their members have attained.

Authority and Jurisdiction

The department of English is not an independent body but a component of a larger organizational whole. As such, its autonomy is limited, its jurisdiction defined by the structure of authority at the institution to which it belongs. In some matters it enjoys the right to govern itself; in others it must abide by the decisions of faculty committees and the administration. The precise degree of autonomy granted the department often determines or influences the kind of program it can offer undergraduates. If it has no power to control the size of its classes, for example, the department may have to forgo certain types of discussion courses and seminars. Or if it is denied the right to exclude students from its program for the major in English, it may have to adapt that program to accommodate students of inferior competence. Determination of the department's authority in these and many other matters is therefore essential to a definition of its role in undergraduate education.

In the classroom and in matters pertaining directly to teaching, the department's authority is all but absolute. Of all departments 77.5 percent enjoy complete autonomy in deciding how courses will be taught (whether as lectures or discussions, for example); another 16.2 percent need only submit their plans to the administration for review. By tradition the classroom is inviolable (a fact that greatly impedes the evaluation of teaching competence and of whole programs, as we shall see), and very few administrators or faculty members from other departments would presume to derogate the department's right to decide just what ought to happen there from day to day. Beyond the classroom, however, the department's rights begin to diminish until finally, in matters involving only the expending of money, the department has no authority at all. Many department chairmen are not told what their subordinates earn; only 0.7 percent of all departments are allowed to establish the salaries they may offer new members. Between the daily conduct of classes, which is the sole prerogative of the teacher, and the general distribution of funds, which is the principal office of the administration, great variation in the power to make decisions may occur. For example, most departments (61.9 percent) have the power to revise their courses as they see fit, but the majority (58.3 percent) may not add or drop a course without administrative approval. Only 8.5 percent have complete autonomy in selecting those they will hire, and even fewer (2.5 percent) may actually appoint new members. The size of the department's normal teaching load is established by various procedures: 10.1 percent of all departments may set their own, 19.6 percent must seek administrative approval, and 29.7 percent are told by the administration how much they will teach. (The rest follow other procedures.) In short, the department is allowed to regulate its own special affairs on most campuses, but its authority is hedged by economic considerations and by its obligation to contribute to the general educational program of the institution to which it belongs.

The amount of authority granted the department varies in direct proportion to the size of the institution. Thus, only 8.4 percent of English departments in small schools have complete autonomy in selecting new staff members, but 19.5 percent of departments in large schools have this power. And only 8.7 percent of departments in small schools are permitted to establish their own teaching loads, but 11.8 percent of departments in large schools may do so. Conversely, some 20 percent of departments in small schools have no voice in decisions on tenure and promotion, whereas only about 2 percent of departments in large schools are thus excluded. No doubt the greater autonomy of large departments may be attributed to the sheer size and organizational complexity of large universities: power must be decentralized and delegated at such institutions, if only because no one person or agency has the time and competence to participate in all the decisions the departments must make. Departments at larger schools thus win a bonus of authority almost by default. It is not clear, however, that their greater freedom to govern themselves inevitably results in better education for undergraduates.

TWO

Staffing Department and Rewarding Faculty

In 1967 the most urgent practical problem facing over half the departments in the nation was how to recruit enough good teachers: 51.3 percent reported that they were having difficulty in staffing their courses. In 1968 the job market changed suddenly and completely. The sellers—those 825 or so graduate students who earn their Ph.D.s in English each year and all others who sought new positions—found jobs extremely scarce, and the buyers—departments in institutions of all kinds and degrees of prestige—found themselves surfeited with applicants. These conditions have not improved in the ensuing years; and now, as everyone knows, the future of the profession looks very grim indeed. This is the most dramatic, the most far-reaching, and the most significant change to occur in the history of college English—a change, it should be noted, imposed from without, not generated by the profession itself. Its causes are not difficult to determine. First, the war in Vietnam drastically altered the nation's economy and greatly reduced the amounts of federal and state funds allocated to education. Inflation, much of which may be attributed to the war, increased costs without increasing tax revenues proportionately. Education thus competed with welfare, medicare, and other expensive domestic programs for what money was left after military spending. The value of endowments and the amounts donated to private institutions decreased as interest rates and taxes rose. Thus, colleges and universities of all kinds have had less money to spend on instruction. Few have created new positions; many have not filled their existing positions.

By a terrible irony, the very war which damaged the economy and diverted funds from higher education also incited rebellion among students; and their violence, or the reports of it, turned many citizens against their colleges and universities. Elected officials like Governor Reagan of California and Governor Meskill of Connecticut, always mistrustful of the academies, could then withhold appropriations, denigrate the faculty, and prevent the further growth of their states' higher educational systems. The full hurt of this "delayed backlash" is only now being felt on the campuses, long after the events which provoked it.

Meanwhile, funds that formerly went to four-year institutions were being diverted to junior and community colleges. The number of two-year colleges has almost tripled in the last decade, at great additional expense to state and local governments. If, as experts predict, the two-year institutions soon will assume responsibility for almost all lower-division instruction, beginning teachers of English may find that most of the available jobs are in two-year colleges—whereas these teachers were trained in graduate school to teach upper-division courses, and most of them would greatly prefer to do so.

It may also be true that for many years the graduate schools were, all unwittingly, producing more Ph.D.s in English than were needed. While the sellers' market prevailed—or was thought to prevail—it seemed certain that the supply of college English teachers was inadequate to meet the demand; indeed, graduate schools were urged to accelerate their programs to remedy a supposed shortage. Allan M. Cartter warned in 1967, however, that "English appears likely to have a surplus [of college teachers] in the 1969–1975 period about sufficient to compensate for deficits in the previous years" (p. 127) and it now appears that his prediction may have been correct. No one can be sure, because no one is certain, even after the panic of 1969 and 1970, just what the demand is or will be. Though college English is not a very large community (its full-time population is only about 21,000), its economy has never been subjected to close and continuous review, its specific needs at any one time never determined. In the spring of 1970 the officers of the MLA assumed this task. They surveyed departments to see how many vacancies were expected, and a year later they inaugurated their efficiently compiled *Job Information Lists,* which have appeared quarterly ever since. Unfortunately, their commendable efforts have served only to reveal how few jobs there are and to intensify competition for those.

Meanwhile, thousands of undergraduates have been discouraged or prevented from entering the profession as graduate schools have reduced their programs in view of the dwindling demand for their products; soon part of a whole generation will have been lost to the profession. Junior faculty members scramble desperately for tenure, and tenure itself has come under attack from young teachers who covet positions now preempted by their elders and from outsiders who demand continuous "accountability" from all faculty members. Only two benefits have resulted from all this economic upheaval: a wider dispersion of teachers just emerging from graduate school (most of whom must now abandon their provincial prejudices and take what jobs they can get) and some salutary reexamination of the profession's motives and practices. The latter may well have been counterbalanced, however, by the craven retreat to security which has marked some departments' response to the new economic pressures. At any rate, these scant benefits must seem cold comfort to those young people who find themselves debarred from the profession of their choice.

I conducted my survey just before the catastrophic trans-
formation of the job market in 1968, and some of the information
on hiring practices I had gathered was rendered obsolete by the
crash. But many of my findings remain pertinent and illuminating.
Thus, much of what I learned about the kinds of competence
departments sought when they were hiring, about hiring at the upper
ranks, about the status of women in the profession, and about
policies on hiring a husband and his wife continues to shed light on
the profession, even though the amount of hiring being done has
greatly diminished. In what follows I shall deal with these matters
separately.

Competencies Sought

Asked to identify those courses they found most difficult to
staff, 29 percent of all departments mentioned linguistics, and 9.5
percent mentioned medieval studies. Other specialties then in demand were freshman English (3.1), the seventeenth century and
Milton (2.7), the eighteenth century (2.7), and the renaissance
(2.3). For the majority (54.2 percent) of departments, however,
recruiting specialists in particular fields was not an urgent problem.
Only a very large department can hope to offer a perfectly comprehensive undergraduate curriculum—one that includes specialized
courses in all fields; and every department—because of the number
of general, introductory, and service courses it is expected to staff—
must enlist the services of many versatile teachers. Although the
convention of identifying a teacher by his specialty is still observed
(and is encouraged by the conventions of graduate study), only
32.3 percent of departments look only for specialists when they have
positions to fill; 20.4 percent look for both specialists and teachers of
general competence, but the majority (53.4 percent) look for
teachers of general ability, without regard to specialties. In other
words, for most departments of English the aim of recruiting (when
they can afford to recruit) is not to acquire a stable of experts but
to enlist a complement of able instructors who are willing to teach
a variety of subjects to undergraduates.

It is appropriate to speculate on the full significance of this
fact. Does it mean that the majority of departments now place

relatively little emphasis on specialization, that although they may list their vacancies by specialties with the MLA, for example, and may discuss candidates' dissertations during interviews, their principal interest is in breadth of mind and teaching skill? And does this mean, in turn, that the courses these departments offer undergraduates may be less narrowly conceived and specialized than some suppose? Two supplementary facts must be considered before these inferences can fairly be drawn; unfortunately, these facts are contradictory in their implications, and thus they complicate rather than clarify our view of the effect of recruiting practices on the state of undergraduate English throughout the land.

The first is that a preference for teachers of general competence is much more common among departments in small colleges than in large universities—and it is at the latter that the great majority of American undergraduates receive their instruction in English. Although 67.1 percent of departments in small schools look for teachers of general competence, only 31 percent of departments in large schools do so. But the 50.6 percent of large departments that seek specialists (the rest look for teachers of both types) have perhaps twice the number of students enrolled in English courses than do the small colleges which prefer teachers of general ability. If we assume that a preference for specialists may result in specialized courses, we may have to conclude that *most* American undergraduates are offered just such courses in English.

On the other hand, an instructor appointed as an expert often is asked to accept teaching assignments well outside his field of specialty. Indeed, so great and various are the demands imposed on departments of English today that very few of their members can be permitted to limit their teaching to a single aspect of their discipline. The man hired as an authority on early-seventeenth-century literature may be needed to teach the popular course in the modern novel—or even to teach freshman English. Here, as in other matters soon to be discussed, whatever impulse the profession may have toward specialism and the nice definition of provinces is thwarted by practical exigencies and the generalized function assigned to the department of English by the academic community. Some may deplore the degree of amateurism that results from this enforced diversification; others may welcome it as an antidote to the insularity and pedantry frequently attributed to English departments in recent years.

Recruiting Senior Teachers

In 1967, during the palmy days of the boom in higher education, there was much talk of wholesale raiding by affluent departments to acquire prominent senior professors. Some envisioned a "vast game of musical chairs," in which celebrated scholars, lured by such inducements as high salaries, reduced teaching loads, and unique library holdings, would move about the country to more and more elevated positions, further and further removed from undergraduate teaching. My investigation revealed, however, that no such grand translation was underway and that relatively little "hiring at the top" was actually occurring among departments of English. Seventy-nine percent of departments reported that they had hired no professors during the *three years* prior to the survey, and 60 percent had hired no associate professors; 8.8 percent had hired one professor, and 23.4 percent one associate professor. Reports from the other end seemed consistent with these figures: 86.3 percent said they had lost no more than one member they wanted to keep. The rate of attrition was slightly higher at small and medium-sized schools than at large institutions (which may mean that the general movement of teachers whose services were in demand was away from the colleges and toward the universities); but if all these reports can be credited, there was relatively little mobility among teachers at the upper ranks even while jobs were plentiful. Now there is almost none. The celebrity hunt of the sixties, which affected only a few persons and departments at most, probably contributed little to the improvement of undergraduate education. The freeze of the seventies, however, has all but eliminated this small but sometimes valuable means of replenishing college departments of English.

The Status of Women

At the time of my survey, well before the movement to effect the liberation of women had gained national prominence, 85.8 percent of all departments flatly asserted that they had no tradition or policy against hiring women. The figure reached 89 percent in large coeducational institutions. About 90 percent of those departments which professed to have no bias against women did in fact have female teachers among the full-time members of their staffs. Among all departments in colleges and universities of all sizes and kinds, the percentage was 84.9; that is, only 15 percent of the English departments in America had no full-time female teachers. (If part-time female teachers were included, the figures would be much higher, of course. Many departments rely on faculty wives and other part-time female employees to staff their freshman programs and their introductory courses.) From these statistics it was possible to conclude that, however well or ill this profession treated women, it did not simply exclude them.

It was more difficult to determine just how women fared in professional competition. Did they receive their fair share of the recognition and rewards the profession had to disburse? More specifically, were they promoted through the ranks as readily as their male colleagues? To answer this question I compiled a mass of statistics, which may be summarized as follows:

Number of English departments with full-time female staff members at each rank. Among departments with women on their staffs, 72.4 percent had female instructors, 77.2 percent had female assistant professors, 46.6 percent had female associate professors, and 43.7 percent had female professors. These figures may be somewhat misleading, however, because they include *all* departments which had *any* women at each rank. More significant are the following statistics:

Average percentage of full-time department members at each rank who were women. What proportion of the department's instructors were females? How many of its professors were males? Here it seemed best to proceed rank by rank. The percentage of women among those who held the rank of instructor varied from about 30 to 40, depending on the size and kind of institution. The average percentage was 37.7. That is, more than a third of all those who taught college English at the lowest rank were women. The average percentage of women at the lowest rank was highest among the very schools most likely to hire women: the large coeducational institutions.

At the rank of assistant professor, which usually signifies some prospect of continued employment, the average percentage of women was 36.1, not much smaller than that for the rank below. It was 47 percent at small, sectarian, noncoeducational institutions, a figure probably explained by the fact that many Catholic colleges of this type are staffed primarily by nuns.

An average of 24.7 percent of college English teachers at the rank of associate professor was women. Once again the percentage for small schools was somewhat higher (25.3 percent), as was that for sectarian (34.4 percent) and noncoeducational (30.3 percent) schools.

As we moved to the top rank, professor, the percentage of women diminished (but not at small, sectarian, noncoeducational schools). The average percentage of professors who were women among all departments was 23.5. At small schools it was 26.4, at medium-sized schools 20.4, and at large schools only 6 percent.

These statistics reveal that—except at a few colleges which, one suspects, employ mostly women (and many of them under vows)—the proportion of females among college teachers of English decreased markedly with elevation in rank. In other words, the higher the rank, the fewer women were to be found.

Percentage of all female teachers who had attained each rank. How many of those women who taught English in college held each rank? An average of 35.5 percent were instructors; almost the same number, 35 percent, were assistant professors; 15.3 percent were associate professors; and 14.2 percent were professors. Among males, 26.4 percent were instructors, 32.2 percent were assistant professors, 19.6 percent associate professors, and 22.2 percent professors. Clearly, the proportion of women in the upper ranks was considerably smaller than the proportion of men; the great majority of women (over 70 percent) were to be found at the lower levels of the hierarchy. This was especially true at the large, public, coeducational institutions, which employ most women.

Do these facts prove that discrimination existed and that women were unfairly denied advancement? That conclusion seems inescapable until one recalls that a larger proportion of women than men drop out of the profession or fail to pursue their careers with full energy. In this sense, the scarcity of women at the upper ranks may be largely voluntary. Feminists would reply, however, that women are often forced to resign or prevented from competing successfully by the profession itself, which discourages them by inconsiderate rules, and by society, which assigns them domestic duties incompatible with full-time teaching. Whatever the truth may be, in the years since my somewhat embarrassing statistics were established, both the profession and society, prodded by the feminists and the federal government, began to reconsider their treatment of women and to take steps to ameliorate their lot. As a result, the MLA's Commission on the Status of Women could express "guarded optimism" in its report of May 1972.

Hiring a Husband and Wife

One plank in the feminist platform, one guideline promulgated by the MLA's Commission calls for the abolition of so-called antinepotism rules, which prohibit departments from hiring married couples. Several arguments are advanced in defense of these rules: (1) That it is difficult to separate the husband's case from his wife's (or vice versa) and therefore it is difficult to judge them individually. If, as sometimes happens, the man proves less able than the woman, to discharge or fail to promote him entails such embarrassment that he may be retained and even advanced, unfairly shielded by his wife. (2) That a husband and wife may vote *en bloc* in departmental affairs (or may seem to do so) and that their power, which sometimes appears to be greater than the sum of its parts, may be resented by other members of the department. (3) That if one member of the husband-and-wife team achieves a position of influence in the department, the other may receive (or seem to receive) favored treatment.

The protectors of women's rights are not impressed by these arguments. They charge, in the words of the MLA commission, that "antinepotism regulations, whether at the university or departmental level, do indeed restrict the employment of women." They will be heartened to learn, therefore, that such rules may not be as common as many people, including the members of the commission, suppose. Only 32.4 percent of departments were forbidden to hire couples in 1967, and the number has diminished since. Another 30 percent reported that they rarely hired couples, seldom had openings for them, or would grant tenure to only one member of a married team. Further analysis of my findings did reveal, however, that antinepotism rules were much more prevalent among large public institutions, which do most of the hiring, than among small colleges: 54.4 percent of the former had them, 20 percent of the latter. It is ironic that large departments, which, because of their very size, are least likely to be captured or disrupted by married couples, are most reluctant to employ them.

Terms of Appointment

Although some institutions may be exploiting the present buyers' market to use and then discard junior faculty members, it is probably still true, as it was in 1967, that the great majority are "hiring to keep." At that time 95.2 percent of all departments assumed that everyone they appointed above the rank of instructor would have full opportunity to achieve promotion and tenure and that each teacher's advancement would depend solely on his own performance. "Failure to meet departmental standards results in dismissal," the officers of the Department of English at Indiana University said. "But this is comparatively rare. . . . New faculty members are appointed with the expectation that they will perform ably (the selection process is thorough), and they usually do."

Those who enter the profession at the rank of assistant professor are usually appointed for an initial period of from one to three years. Almost all one-year contracts are renewed after a term's service and are continued on a year-to-year basis until a three-year contract is awarded or until the first decision on promotion and tenure is reached. Departments that offer three-year appointments to new members often renew them after two and a half years, without awarding promotion or tenure; decision on these matters is usually made after four and a half years. There are many variations on these patterns. At the University of California, Berkeley, new members remain assistant professors for eight years, but they are advised in their fourth year whether or not it is probable that they will be retained and promoted. At the University of California, San Diego, the usual term as assistant professor is six years; but each case must be reviewed by a faculty committee every two years, so that the candidate will be regularly and fully apprised of his status. The most common period of service as assistant professor is five years, and it is now the practice of many departments to offer those who will not be retained a terminal year in which to seek employment elsewhere. On the other hand, early promotions are sometimes awarded to especially promising young teachers whose services their departments are anxious to keep.

Tenure

The practice of assuring college teachers security of employment has now become almost universal, and achieving tenure has become, for better or for worse, a primary goal of many who enter the profession. Of all four-year colleges and universities, 91.3 percent grant tenure. The figure varies considerably among schools of different types—it is 97.1 percent for public institutions, 91.5 percent for private, and only 82.9 percent for sectarian schools; but institutions that make no provision for tenure are now in a small minority. The widespread acceptance of the concept of tenure can be attributed in large measure, of course, to the militant efforts of the American Association of University Professors, whose policy on tenure provides a standard for the profession. That policy is stated, in part, as follows: "After the expiration of a probationary period, teachers or investigators should have permanent or continuous tenure. . . . Beginning with appointment to the rank of full-time instructor or a higher rank, the probationary period should not exceed seven years, including within this period full-time service in all institutions of higher education" (*AAUP Bulletin,* Summer 1967, p. 247).

Thirty-two percent of all institutions have simply adopted this policy as their own; 44 percent have even more liberal policies (that is, decision on tenure is reached before the seventh year); 2.9 percent award tenure with promotion; and the rest have various other policies (including the 8.7 percent that do not grant formal tenure). Those who approve of tenure as an institution (and good arguments against it can be advanced) will applaud the fact that more than three quarters of all institutions offering four-year programs in English now subscribe to the AAUP's policy or have more liberal policies of their own. Among large public institutions, which employ about 55 percent of all college teachers of English, 88 percent meet the AAUP's standards, and well over half of them exceed those standards.

At 43.7 percent of all institutions, the decision to award or to deny tenure is, in effect, a decision to retain or to dismiss the candidate. If faculty members do not achieve tenure within the various periods these institutions stipulate, they are not rehired. But almost exactly the same number, 43.3 percent, have no such policy of "up or out." (The rest retain on a year-to-year basis or seldom need to make this decision.) Where policies on tenure are most liberal—at large public institutions—the decision on tenure is most often crucial to the career of the candidate.

Deciding on Tenure and Promotion

At approximately 12 percent of all institutions, the power to decide who will be granted tenure and who will be promoted resides with the administration alone; the departments have no vote in the matter. (As noted earlier, many more small colleges than large are ruled from the top: about 20 percent of departments in the small schools lack authority in matters of tenure and promotion, but only about 2 percent of departments in large schools are denied such authority.) At all other institutions, however, departments must establish procedures for making recommendations to the administrative officers who have final responsibility for awarding tenure and promotion. Most of these departments (91 percent, to be exact) follow the same procedure for tenure as for promotion; many decide cases of both types together. The most common procedures may be listed according to the degrees of democratization they imply. (The numbers in parentheses indicate the percentage of departments which subscribe to each procedure. The first number is for tenure; the second for promotion.)

1. Decisions are made by the chairman alone. (42.8, 44.6)

2. Decisions are made by the chairman in consultation (often informal) with other members of the department. (3.6, 4.5)

3. Decisions are made by the chairman and an advisory committee appointed by him. (21, 22.7)

4. Decisions are made by all those superior in rank to the candidate. (9.8, 10.8)

5. Decisions are made by a committee elected by the tenured members of the department or, in a few cases, by the department as a whole. (6.5, 7.1)

In well over 40 percent of all departments, then, decisions on tenure and promotion are made by the chairman without formal consultation with his colleagues. This most autocratic, least democratic procedure is more common in small schools than in large: the percentages of departments in small colleges which entrust the power of decision to the chairman are 44.7 and 47.8; in large universities they are 37.9 and 34.1; conversely, the percentages of small departments in which such decisions are made by several members are 18.6 and 19.2, of large departments 59.8, and 64.7. Here again we observe that, probably for practical reasons, authority is more widely distributed in large institutions than in small.

Having arrived at its decisions, the department must communicate them to those who represent the institution as a whole in final deliberations on tenure and promotion. (The approval of the trustees or regents is usually granted automatically.) Some institutions follow elaborate procedures at this point. The English department as Wesleyan University, for example, must first submit its recommendations to the president's advisory committee, which, if it agrees, passes them on to the president; then his decisions are reviewed by the academic council (consisting of all faculty members with the rank of professor), which must approve the president's recommendations by a majority vote. At Indiana University the chairman notifies the dean of the college of the department's decisions; that officer appoints a secret committee, whose judgments are then submitted to the dean of the faculty; he appoints another secret committee, which can initiate promotions as well as deny them; its decisions are then transmitted to the president for approval. Most institutions, however, reach their final decisions by one of the following less tortuous routes. (Numbers are percentages of departments following each procedure.)

1. The department makes recommendation to the president, who decides. (5.8)

2. The department makes recommendation to the dean, who makes recommendation to the president. (31)

3. The department makes recommendation to a general faculty committee, which advises the president. (14.3)

4. The department makes recommendation to a general faculty committee, which advises the dean, who advises the president. (19.4)

Of the remaining 30 percent, 20.9 follow variations on these procedures, 5.4 percent do not know how decisions on tenure and promotion are made at their institutions, and 3.3 have no fixed procedures. Clearly, the second procedure listed above is the most common; once again, finer analysis discloses that the simpler procedures are more common among smaller institutions.

The administration always accedes to the department's recommendations on tenure and promotion at 18.3 percent of all schools; at another 63 percent, it usually does. Less than 10 percent of all departments report that their administrations regularly reject their recommendations. One must conclude, then, that on most campuses the professional fates of young teachers of English are usually decided in the councils of the senior members of the department.

Criteria

How are those councils conducted, and what standards are applied as candidates for tenure and promotion are judged? No business on the department's agenda is more delicate or more demanding of wisdom; none is of greater moment, both to the candidates and to the department as a whole. As they define the criteria by which they will decide the cases that come before them, as they elect to value one professional activity or personal attribute above another, those charged with making the department's recommendations on matters of tenure and promotion are, in effect, expressing a concept of the English teacher and his function. They are saying, either explicitly or by implication, "This is what the department wants and will reward," and in saying that they come as close as most departments ever do to defining their understanding of what they are about.

When asked to list their criteria for tenure and promotion in order of importance, most departments (66.5 percent) declare that they value most highly the ability to teach well, and no other competence or professional accomplishment is deemed more important by an appreciable number of departments. Scholarship—and, in most instances, published evidence of that achievement—is ranked second: 25 percent of departments place it second on their lists of criteria, 10.4 place it first. Next comes service to the institution (administrative duties or work on college-wide committees, for example), which is ranked first by 1.9 percent of departments, second by 15.1 percent, and third by most of the rest. Length of service, professional service (usually through national organizations), personality, promise of growth, and service to students are also mentioned, in that order of frequency. Many departments consider all but the first three qualifications—teaching competence, scholarship, and service to the institution—to be of minor importance. Outstanding professional service, for example, may enhance the candidate's reputation, but he will not be promoted for that achievement alone. Some departments require evidence of distinction in at least two of the first three categories. Thus, a candidate may be excused for contributing relatively little to college affairs if he is known to be a skillful teacher and a productive scholar. But it is in deciding precisely how much weight to assign to scholarly activity —and, more specifically, to publication—that departments differ most widely and most significantly.

A very few, like the Department of English at the University of California, Berkeley, place primary emphasis on scholarship and will not award tenure or promotion unless the candidate has produced a sufficient body of published material which is judged to be of good quality. "Superb teaching may help a man's case," said one officer of that department, "but we assume that we all teach well, and therefore we don't promote people just because they are good teachers." At the opposite extreme are those institutions—most of them small colleges—at which publication is actually discouraged because it is thought to distract from teaching. The

remaining departments that have well-defined policies on this
matter—and most do not—take positions somewhere between these
poles. In general, small departments and departments that do not
offer graduate programs are more likely than medium-sized or
large departments to value teaching ability over scholarly accomplishment. In other words, the degree to which the department
rewards scholarly productivity (or demands evidence of such
productivity) is directly proportional, in most instances, to its size
and to the size of its curriculum. It is also proportional to the incidence of Ph.D.s among members of the department; the higher the
percentage of Ph.D.s, the greater the emphasis on scholarship and
publication. But modifications and qualifications of strict policies
on publication are common as chairmen and their advisors try to
reconcile competing requirements for advancement in ways suitable
to the circumstances they confront. Here are some statements they
made in interviews:

*I suppose we are more impressed by publications than by reports of
good teaching. An article or a book is a tangible object, which sits on
a shelf; teaching just occurs, and its quality is hard to measure.*

*We believe that a man either publishes or perishes inwardly. "Great
teachers" wear out fast.*

*Before we grant tenure, we insist that the candidate submit evidence
that he can write and write well. But the evidence may be a poem or
an unpublished article. We just want to make sure he can use words
effectively.*

*Many scholarly articles and books published in our field today are
almost worthless. They contribute very little to the improvement of
education, which is what we are after.*

*We are about to dismiss one young man who has published a great deal
but who has done nothing for us. He is just using the department.*

*We want our people to publish if they can because it may do them—
and the department—some good.*

Some chairmen are convinced that their department's national
reputation depends almost entirely on the number of articles and
books produced by its members, that the department will soon
become "invisible" and will find it difficult to impress those who

disburse funds if its name does not appear on the final pages of a sufficient number of articles or on the title pages of enough books. Others deplore the fact that the need to publish compels some faculty members to slight or to avoid entirely such arduous teaching assignments as freshman English. Said one chairman, "Some of the young men tell me, 'I can't read all those papers, because I won't have time for my own work.' I ask them, 'What is your work if it isn't teaching students to write?' " In his department as in others, however, eligibility for tenure and promotion is often measured not according to how many lower-division classes the candidate has been willing to assume but according to whether his published works have enhanced the department's prestige.

English teachers regularly require their students to "publish" (that is, to express their thoughts and discoveries in formal written utterances), and they do so in part because they believe that the act of conception is not completed until the thing conceived is issued or made public. One enlightened view of scholarly publication now endorsed by many departments follows from this belief. It holds that teachers must continue to read and to make their own discoveries in order to teach well, and its presumes that most teachers will want to share what they have found with others. It concedes that some faculty members may "publish" best by communicating to students in the classroom. It also recognizes, however, that many will find their fit audience only among their peers, who are best addressed through journals for scholars; it therefore commends (though it does not demand) efforts fully to realize fine perceptions by giving them precise expression and then submitting them to the judgments of others who are expert. If, as those who take this view assume, faculty members teach best what they have struggled to express in writing, scholarly publication of the kind these departments encourage should complement and enrich the teaching of undergraduates.

Evaluating Teaching

Only a few teachers of English publish significant works during their professional careers, and many publish no works at all; the daily business and sole occupation of most of them is teaching. It is on their teaching alone, therefore, that most members of this profession must be judged, and it is for evidences of good or at least satisfactory teaching that most departments look as they conduct their periodic reviews of staff members.

Very few other professions subject their members to such frequent and such crucial evaluation; the stockbroker, for example, is not appointed for a term of service which leads to a critical review of his competence and to possible dismissal. (Ironically, it is the military that most closely resembles college teaching in its practice of ranking and regularly reassessing its members.) For all its show of system, however, the teaching profession's judgments of its members' competence and effectiveness at their primary task are no more precise and well founded than those of other professions. Indeed, they may be less so, because it is peculiarly difficult to define the criteria and to certify the evidence on which its judgments must be based.

When confronted with the central question "What constitutes good teaching?" some departments (or their spokesmen) are simply unable or unwilling to answer. No doubt they believe they have experienced good teaching and can recognize it when they see it, but they decline to reduce so complex and various a phenomenon to formula or definition. Others are willing to undertake at least a summary description of the effective teacher and his art, and it is possible to identify certain abilities and attributes to which large numbers of them refer as they try their hands at this difficult task. The skills and characteristics most frequently mentioned when English teachers are asked to define good teaching are stimulation, motivation (cited in 86.3 percent of all replies); knowledge, mastery of subject (76.9 percent); enthusiasm, interest (40.2); rapport with students (39.3); fresh ideas, critical insights (34.6); responsibility in meeting classes and professional duties (19.2); high, fair standards (18.8); and popularity with students (3.9). Other attributes mentioned, but less frequently, are consideration for the varying abilities of students; skill in relating contents of courses to other aspects of students' lives; sense of humor. It would be wrong to attribute great significance to such a list, however, because it represents a distillation of a number of necessarily brief and superficial responses to the question "What are your criteria for good teaching?"

It could be argued that when they are faced with such a whopping query, most respondents are likely simply to produce a string of those virtues to which the profession gives lip service. Even such a catalog may be revealing, however, if only because it probably indicates which qualities and abilities departments believe they ought to respect and reward. A composite picture derived from a representative sample of responses to this question describes the model teacher as one who stimulates his students and inspires strong motivation in them by conveying, with enthusiasm and consideration of their interests and needs, an understanding of a subject he knows well. He is one who has original perceptions, an abiding interest in his subject, and the ability to communicate both of these to his students so that they will want to join him in the rigorous but imaginative pursuit of his discipline. And, finally, he is one who meets his professional responsibilities punctually and efficiently. Variations, amplifications, and clarifications of this paragon (which inevitably reads a bit like the Boy Scout Creed) may be offered, and none will comprehend all teachers at all institutions. Moreover, use of such terms as "stimulate," "understanding," and "imaginative" may raise more problems of definition than they solve. But if a generalized description of the good teacher is wanted, so that the great blanks it contains can be filled in as each case is judged, some such loose definition may serve. It then devolves to individual departments to match this idealization, or some model of their own, with what evidence of the teacher's actual performance they can obtain.

Precisely at this point, however, a major problem arises, one which plagues most departments and to which few have found satisfactory solutions. It is the problem of just how to obtain reliable and accurate evidence of what actually occurs in each instructor's classroom. This profession is unique in that the very scene of its primary activity is considered inviolable, and the product of its principal labor cannot readily be measured. The college teacher is seldom or never observed at his work except by those on whom he is working, and the effects of his efforts cannot be collected to be assessed. Those who are charged with judging his competence as a teacher must therefore gather their evidence by indirect, imperfect means, and often the evidence they acquire is of dubious validity.

The most common means to which they resort are listed below. (Figures indicate what percentage of all departments use each procedure; many, of course, use more than one.)

1. Informal personal contacts. (93.4)

2. Reviews of assignments, examinations, and other teaching materials. (50.9)

3. Student evaluations solicited by the department or by the administration. (39.9)

4. Classroom visits. (36.2)

5. Informal contacts with students. (28.0)

6. Student evaluations published independently by students. (18.8)

Other means or types of evidence reported include opinions of colleagues (including colleagues in other departments) solicited by the department or the administration; regular evaluation sessions; informal, unsolicited student evaluations; informal discussions within the department; comparison of how well the teacher's students perform on common examinations; review of grades given by teacher; comparison of class enrollments; the teacher's performance as a lecturer in sectioned courses; his performance in giving oral examinations; his performance in departmental meetings; advisors' reports on students' preferences; interviews with students changing majors.

With so many sources and kinds of information available to them, it might seem that those who must judge teaching ability should have little difficulty in arriving at a just estimate of each instructor's performance. All of the most common practices afford abundant occasions for error, however, and none ensures certainty or even near certainty. The virtues and limitations of the several procedures may be summarized as follows:

Informal Personal Contacts. Impressions of the candidate's traits and abilities gathered over several years of professional association with him are bound to condition the judgments of those who must decide whether he deserves tenure or promotion. Some departments rely entirely on such informal impressions, using no other means to determine teaching competence. They believe that from his contributions to departmental shoptalk, from his remarks about his students, from his comments on literature and other matters which pertain to his discipline, even from his behavior on social occasions one may come to know the cast of a man's mind, and deduce (or guess) with reasonable accuracy how he must conduct his classes. They assume, many of them, that there is nothing deeply mysterious about the teaching process and that if a man demonstrates wit, imagination, learning, and compassion in his conversations with his colleagues he will probably retain those attributes when he addresses his students, will probably teach well. Finally, they suppose that any gross discrepancy between his performance inside the classroom and out will eventually become known. Thus, these departments put their faith in their ability to judge their members as human beings and to predict, more or less intuitively, which human beings will make good teachers and which will not.

The chief objections to this procedure—or lack of procedure —for estimating teaching skill are: (1) That it is entirely *too* haphazard and imprecise. Those who are responsible for judging the candidate's competence as a teacher may misinterpret his personal style, make mistaken inferences, or be unduly influenced by some insignificant mannerism or act. The judges' subjective impressions of the candidate's daily behavior as a man must be translated into some notion of his conduct in the classroom, and this may be a highly fallible practice. (2) That it is impossible for senior members of large departments to know well all those they must judge; therefore, they must depend in many cases on hearsay and rumor. (3) That this procedure encourages politicking and the courting of favor and penalizes candidates who are incapable of making themselves personally attractive to those who will decide their fates. The lot of the young teacher who will be judged on his personality alone, without regard to formal evidence of his performance in the classroom, is especially precarious in those departments—and there are several—which are riven with feuds. As a senior member of one such department said, "At this place a man's teaching career can be ruined if he walks to the library with the wrong colleague." (4) That it may become impossible to deny tenure and promotion, whether or not they are deserved, simply because no objective evidence of incompetence is available. "We might as well give them tenure when we hire them," said an officer of the English department at one of the California state colleges, "because even after five years we don't have any way to prove that they are not entitled to it."

Reviews of Teaching Materials. Most teachers of English have occasion to distribute printed exercises, assignments, examinations, and reading lists to their students, and often these documents provide valuable clues to how they conceive and conduct their courses. A lazy, hackneyed assignment ("Write a paper on women in Shakespeare's plays") may be indicative of unimaginative or cynical teaching. A fresh and ingenious examination question, well designed to test both knowledge and critical ability, is presumptive evidence of teaching skill. Some departments now require candidates for tenure and promotion to submit examples of their teaching materials when their cases are to be judged; these are evaluated just as scholarly publications are appraised. If it is remembered that there is more to teaching than preparing impressive handouts, there seems to be no danger in this procedure and much to be gained from it.

Student Evaluations. As American college students have become more assertive in recent years and as faculty members, administrators, and governing boards have become more sensitive to their opinions and demands, one instrument for measuring teaching skill which had long been neglected or disparaged, the student evaluation or rating of teachers and their courses, has suddenly enjoyed a great vogue. To invite or to entertain students' comments on their teachers is not an innovation, of course: a number of institutions—among them the University of Washington, Bennington College, and Georgia Institute of Technology—have had such procedures for years; at others—Harvard University and the University of Michigan, for example—the students themselves have been publishing their ratings since the twenties. Now, however, it appears that the need to establish a medium which will permit students to express their views of their instructors is felt on almost every campus in the land. Although John W. Gustad reported in 1967 (p. 271) that "use of student ratings as a technique (of evaluation) has declined substantially during the past five years" among chairmen and deans, I found that 50.9 percent of all departments of English were then consulting formal reports of student opinion at some point during their discussion of candidates for tenure and promotion. Not all credited them highly, but there was a general feeling that they should not be ignored entirely.

Three formal means are used to collect students' opinions of their teachers:

1. Individual teachers may request students to evaluate them and their courses. The results may be communicated to others (for example, to the chairman of the department), but they seldom are, either because they are unfavorable to the teacher or because he is reluctant to brag. No doubt teachers may gain self-understanding from such private surveys, but they are under little external pressure to act on criticisms and suggestions thus obtained and may simply file them away.

2. The department or the administration may solicit student evaluations by distributing questionnaires to all those enrolled in the teacher's courses, to recent graduates, or to both. At some institutions (for example, the University of Washington), the administration simply makes its surveying facilities available to instructors, who may or may not forward the findings to their superiors. At others, students' opinions are collected by the department or the administration, shown to the instructor if he wishes, and reviewed when decisions on tenure and promotion are made. To ensure that all constituencies of the institution are represented in the surveying process, students and faculty members at Occidental College have collaborated to compose an excellent questionnaire, which is distributed in all classes. Responses are collected by the department chairman but not examined until final grades have been recorded. The chairman discusses the student evaluations with the instructors, then keeps a record of the ratings. This record is consulted by the dean and the advisory council (an elected body) when they make what are in effect final decisions on tenure and promotion. Laura Kent (1967, p. 323) reports yet another procedure, which has been developed at Montana State College:

There, student ratings are kept on a voluntary basis and are seen by the instructor only, although names of instructors requesting ratings are listed in the dean's office and are available to the Curricula and

Instruction Committee. Moreover, "any instructor who does not volun-
tarily submit himself to appraisal may be asked to do so by the students
of his class"; if at least 20 percent of the class petitions the student
section of the Curricula and Instruction Committee, and if the claim
is determined to be valid, the chairman of the student section notifies
"both the instructor and his department head of the class request."
Although these provisions do not say that the faculty member must
submit himself to evaluation, he is obviously under considerable pres-
sure to do so.

It is clear that under these rules the threat of student evaluation
may become a kind of coercive device.

3. The students themselves may have had some such aim
when they first began to publish their own ratings of their teachers.
These "guides to teachers and courses" are now available on many
campuses, including the University of California at Berkeley and
Santa Barbara, the University of Wisconsin, and Bryn Mawr, to
name but a few. They range in quality from snide, even vicious
"exposés" to highly responsible, well-prepared critiques. The best
of them offer helpful course descriptions not available in the official
catalog, as well as carefully compiled ratings (which are sometimes
correlated with the grades the respondents received). So great is
the popularity of such evaluations that the National Student Association now publishes a "student's confidential guide" to preparing
confidential guides!

It takes a bit of courage for faculty members to express
opposition to student evaluations, if only because those who do so
may be suspected of being poor losers in a popularity poll. Nevertheless, many teachers, good and bad, remain honestly skeptical
about the value of student ratings. A few—probably a dwindling
minority today—openly challenge the students' right to criticize
their superiors in age and wisdom. Others argue that to subject the
instructor to such criticism is to demean him and to threaten his
integrity; the teacher, they say, is compromised when he must sell
himself or cater to student opinion. But the most common objection
to student evaluation concerns the competence of the evaluators and
the means by which their opinions are gathered and interpreted.
Although recent investigations have shown that students are not as
easily duped by classroom histrionics and lenient grading as faculty

members suppose, their competence to judge their instructor's scholarship or "command of his subject" is obviously limited by their inexperience. No one knows better than they whether the instructor has succeeded in "inspiring strong motivation in them" (to recall our description of the ideal teacher) or in communicating his perceptions and his interest in his subject, but as learners they are not well qualified to assess their teacher's learning. Therefore, if their ratings are to be pure expressions of the best evidence they have to offer—that which reveals something about what has happened at their end of the educational process—they should not be asked to pretend to an expertise they do not have. Those items on the standard questionnaire which request students to rate their instructor's erudition or "mastery of his subject" invite invalid responses; when these responses are combined with replies to questions on the instructor's appearance, his mannerisms, and his fairness to students (as they are at the University of Connecticut and elsewhere), the conglomerate rating which results may be seriously misleading.

Furthermore, too few institutions acknowledge by their procedures for assessing student evaluations that, no matter how they distribute and retrieve their questionnaires (or no matter how the survey is conducted by the students themselves), they are *taking a sample* of student opinion, not collecting the opinions of all students. Administrators and departmental offices often point to tabulations of the students' replies and say, "That is what the students think." What they should say, of course, is "This is what some students think when confronted with these questions, and their opinions may or may not be representative." Unless great care is taken to elicit a high percentage of responses from a properly selected sample of the student body, the findings may be completely invalid or perfectly ambiguous. If all members of an instructor's class are asked to evaluate his teaching, for example, and only 50 percent return their questionnaires, a sample *has* been taken (statisticians call it a "self-selecting sample"); but there is no way to determine whether that sample is representative. Why did one half of the class respond and not the other? Are the opinions collected those of the dedicated and the cooperative or those of the enthusiastic and the disgruntled? Often the ratings are expressed numerically, which may lend a spurious appearance of quantifiable fact to what is actually a crude computation of random opinion on a highly complex subject. If the "fact" is then entered on the teacher's record and given great credence and weight when that record is judged, the instructor may be done a disservice, his professional career blighted by false or tainted evidence.

Interviews with college teachers of English at all ranks in all parts of the country suggest that most of them are willing to entertain their students' criticisms, complaints, and suggestions. Very few have any desire simply to talk to themselves in the classroom; many are anxious to enlist their students' collaboration in improving their courses. What disturbs them most is not the prospect of being evaluated but the slipshod methods by which students' opinions are now gathered, reported, and construed.

Classroom Visitation. Despite the tradition which holds that to invade a man's class for the purpose of observing his teaching is to violate his professional rights, senior members regularly visit the classes of junior members in a surprising number—over a third— of the departments of English in American colleges and universities, and most of those who subscribe to this practice are convinced that it is the only fair and reliable way to evaluate teaching ability. At Marquette University, for example, the chairman and members of an advisory committee visit each new member's classes at least twice a year during the first two years of his appointment. They believe that both the instructors and the department benefit from this procedure. They say that they can easily identify the obviously incompetent and the obviously brilliant teachers among their junior staff and are better prepared to dismiss the former and reward the latter. At Wellesley College, classes taught by instructors and assistant professors are observed twice a year by two or three senior faculty members, who sometimes visit as a team. Apparently this procedure causes little or no dissension in this small but relatively congenial department, although the value of the visits is doubted by many of its members. At Dartmouth College every new member of the department is assigned to a senior member, who serves as his "mentor"; they visit each other's classes, and the counselor reports to the department on the junior member's teaching. And at Western Illinois University the senior observer has been replaced by a television camera: videotapes of "live classes" are reviewed and discussed by the instructor and the chairman. This practice is said to be "most constructive."

The principal argument against classroom visits is that the presence of the observer, whether human or electronic, inevitably affects the observed, and therefore what the official examiner witnesses is not a representative specimen of the instructor's teaching but a special performance staged for a special occasion. If the class goes badly, it may be necessary to attribute this ill success to the instructor's nervousness under scrutiny; if it goes well, the visitor may suspect that the instructor has prepared it with unusual care—has even, perhaps, rehearsed it—and that his students are rallying to his support with unwonted loyalty and enthusiasm. In any case, the observer can never say, "This is how this man teaches." Indeed, the evidence he collects may be as partial and fallible as that collected by indirect means. It is also argued that visitation may do harm to young teachers and that it demands an unwarranted amount of the visitor's time. Certainly it would require great amounts of senior members' time to visit the classes of all the young teachers in large departments. Because they cannot afford the expense it entails, because they are reluctant to offend or to inhibit their junior colleagues, and because they are skeptical of the value of visitation, most departments forgo this most obvious means of investigating teaching competence.

In 1965 an ad hoc committee of the Yale faculty which was appointed to review that university's procedures for awarding tenure and promotion came to the melancholy conclusion that "the problem of evaluating teaching is one for which no solution seems altogether satisfactory." Most departments of English would concur. Many of them have tried some or all of the solutions rehearsed above and have found them unsatisfactory for some or all of the reasons given. Each procedure interposes a filter of one kind or another between the judges and the complex phenomenon they are asked to judge. Nor is it likely that they would judge much more wisely if they could view the phenomenon directly: the learning (and hence the teaching) process is as yet so imperfectly understood that absolute standards for measuring teaching effectiveness seem unattainable at present. Finally, most departments are forced to admit, to themselves and to higher authorities, that they simply cannot *certify* the teaching competence of any of their members, can only estimate or divine how well each performs in the classroom. They may console themselves that, as one department chairman put it "it's pretty hard to hide really *bad* teaching" and may assume that, if there are no serious complaints, most members of the department must be teaching satisfactorily. But precisely how much each is accomplishing and how well their total program is succeeding they can never be quite sure, and that uncertainty may debilitate or vitiate much of their enterprise. There is a certain specific sense in which this profession simply does not know what it is doing.

THREE

Departmental Governance

Chairmanship

In 78.1 percent of all English departments the chief officer is called a chairman; in almost all the remaining he is called a head. (One relatively new department, that at the University of California, Santa Cruz, has adopted the fine Canadian term *convener*.) In some instances the two titles designate different offices with different degrees of authority. Thus, New York University, which has two campuses, has two departments of English, each of which has a chairman; presiding over both is a head. The term *head* formerly implied that the power to make most final decisions within the department was vested in the chief officer; the term *chairman* implied that the chief officer's powers were limited and subject to democratic review. This distinction has now been blurred, however, and the choice of titles no longer provides an infallible clue to the distribution of power within the department. Eventually the two titles may become synonomous and interchangeable.

The chairman is elected by his fellow members of the English department at 7.5 percent of all institutions; elsewhere he is selected by the president of the institution or his administrative officers, with or without the advice and consent of the department. In this matter as in others, departments in large schools enjoy a somewhat higher degree of autonomy than those in medium-sized or small schools, but relatively few departments of all sizes are *formally* consulted by the administration when a new chairman is to be appointed. Among those that are consulted is the department of English at the University of Chicago, where a lengthy procedure ensures that all interests will be represented. There the dean inaugurates the process of selection by convening the whole department under the temporary chairmanship of a senior professor. A committee of three is elected to consult with every member of the department and to recommend a candidate. The whole department then votes on this recommendation, which is forwarded to the dean whether or not it is approved by the department. If there is disagreement within the department, the dean appoints an ad hoc committee to resolve the dispute. He then forwards his recommendation to the provost, who makes recommendation to the president. Most administrators are unwilling simply to impose a chairman on the department; most elicit the opinions, nominations, and recommendations of the faculty, if only through informal conferences. At almost all schools, however, the administration reserves the final right to decide who will serve as the officer accountable to it for the conduct of the department.

At about 70 percent of all institutions, the chairman is appointed to serve for an indefinite period. When a term is set, the most popular is three years. Large departments are more likely than small ones to limit the chairman's term of office. At 94.2 percent of the institutions that limit the chairman's term, he may be reappointed. Thus, the chairman of the English department at Brown University is appointed by the president to serve four years, but if all goes well he may be asked to remain in office for at least one more term. "Nowadays it is difficult to find a good man who is willing to take the job," said one officer of the department, "and we are inclined to keep anyone who handles it satisfactorily."

The chairmanship is rotated—that is, regularly reassigned among the senior members—in 14.6 percent of all departments. This procedure is said to distribute the burden of the office more equitably and to prevent the autocratic acquisition of power. In large departments, however, the duties of the chairman have become so specialized, so complex, and so demanding that only a few members can or will undertake them; thus, rotation often is not feasible. As the chairman comes more and more to resemble a business executive, serving in this capacity may become a profession in itself.

The distinction and responsibilities which accrue to the chairman are acknowledged by a special stipend at 29.6 percent of all institutions; the man who becomes chairman is automatically awarded a bonus of from 10 to 20 percent of his salary. Some administrative officers argue that this is a bad practice. "They get used to higher living and won't give up the job," the provost at an eastern university said. The answer to this objection is best illustrated by the English department at the University of Pennsylvania, where an extra stipend is attached both to the chairmanship and to the assistant chairmanship. It is well understood that these positions are temporary and that those who occupy them will be awarded the added wage only while they serve. Other members of the department may earn extra money by such extraprofessional activities as writing textbooks and reviewing; the time-consuming office of chairman should also be rewarded, it is said, but that reward should be relinquished with the office.

The only practical reward most chairmen receive, however, is a reduction in their teaching schedules; 58.2 percent of all departments afford their chairmen some relief from the normal teaching load. Paradoxically, the lighter the regular teaching load, the greater the reduction for the chairman is likely to be. Among chairmen of all departments (including those which reduce the chairman's load and those which do not) the most common load is nine hours. Very few chairmen do no teaching at all; even those who must direct the multifarious activities of large departments usually prefer to maintain contact with students and their professional skills by teaching at least one class each academic year.

The duties of the chairman often include such onerous tasks as recruiting, management of the department's fiscal affairs, assignment of courses, housekeeping, review of candidates for tenure and promotion, and participation in the many meetings at which the department's educational policies are formulated. Chairmen of several large departments have found that one man cannot perform all these duties satisfactorily, that some or many of them must be delegated to subordinates. Of all departments, 15 percent now appoint (or elect) an assistant (or associate or vice) chairman, who relieves the chief officer of a number of his administrative chores.

In institutions with more than 8,000 undergraduates, over 50 percent of the English departments appoint an assistant chairman. In about 80 percent of all cases he is appointed for an indefinite period, but some departments limit his term of office to two, three, or four years. Only 16.6 percent of those institutions which make provision for an assistant chairman attach an extra stipend to the position, but in most his teaching load is reduced, frequently to six hours. Whether the assistant chairman succeeds the chairman when the latter retires from office depends on local contingencies and traditions: at some universities it is understood that the assistant chairman is an apprentice chairman; at others the office is rotated and no such presumption obtains.

If it is difficult to find distinguished teachers who are willing to accept the chairmanship—and several departments which have recently conducted lengthy searches report that it is—the reason may be not only that the position entails a great deal of tedious and sometimes depressing labor but also that it demands rival, almost antithetical abilities and temperaments. On the one hand, the chairman is expected to be an efficient administrator, who combines managerial skill with political acumen. On the other he is expected to be an outstanding scholar and teacher, who can elicit his colleagues' respect. Perhaps because they despair of finding all these virtues in one man and because they value orderly administration above all else, many departments no longer consider it essential that the chairman have a national reputation as a scholar and teacher. Only 25.7 percent of the departments continue to look for outstanding scholarship and teaching ability in their chairmen;

33.5 percent now conceive the office primarily as an administrative position. The rest settle for some compromise.

The majority view of the chairman's power and function is consistent with this more modest view of the qualities he must bring to the office. Apparently the days are over when the chairman was a kind of benevolent despot who formed the department in his own image and ruled rather than chaired. Only 6.2 percent of all departments report that their chairmen are independent leaders who control their departments from the top; 31.4 percent declare that their chairmen are merely presiding officers or spokesmen for their departments, but the great majority—65 percent—say that their chairmen are both. That is, the chairman's function in almost two thirds of all departments is to lead the department in the democratic conduct of its affairs. Often a distinction is made between the chairman's role within the department and his role outside. Among his colleagues he may be little more than a "convener" or referee, who must abide by the decisions of the majority. When he confronts the faculty senate or the administration on the department's behalf, however, he must appear to *be* the department as he fights to protect its interests and to present its point of view. In some departments, most of them small, a further distinction is made between decisions pertaining to personnel, which are made by the chairman alone, and decisions pertaining to academic programs and educational policy, which are reached by democratic procedures. In any case, the status of the chairman in most of today's departments of English is best described by a paradox: he is "the first among equals," one who governs by arranging for others to govern.

Committees

The department is governed by the whole of its membership at 79.8 percent of all institutions. When major changes in their programs are contemplated or other important matters are to be discussed, the chairmen of these fully democratized departments may prepare agenda and present proposals, but decisions are reached by open discussion and majority vote at plenary meetings. Most (90.7 percent) small departments conduct their business in this way, and the chairmen of those departments often can determine consensus simply by polling their colleagues informally. Large departments—say, the 28 percent with more than twenty members —must follow more cumbersome, parliamentary procedures. Regular meetings must be scheduled (most commonly once a month), and much of the department's business must be delegated to committees. Although 31.7 percent of all departments have no committees of any kind, most of these are small and together employ no more than 20 percent of the profession. The remaining 80 percent of all college English teachers are probably doomed to serve on departmental committees at some time during their professional careers.

The most common number of committees among small and medium-sized departments is one to three; among large departments, four to six. Often these include an executive committee, which has multiple duties and broad powers, as well as standing committees, whose deliberations concern a single segment of the department's program (for example, freshman English) or single but recurrent problems (for example, liaison with the library). The executive committee, often elected and constituted to ensure that all ranks are represented, advises the chairman on matters of policy (on which the department as a whole may vote eventually) and relieves him of some administrative tasks; 15.3 percent of all departments (but 31.7 percent of large departments) have such supercommittees. The most common standing committees are freshman English (found at 53.5 percent of all institutions), library (32 percent), graduate (29.1), curriculum (28.7), honors (21.1), major (20.7), and teacher education (14.5).

The committee structure of a very large department may be illustrated by the following list of the major committees which the department of English at Indiana University (which had seventy full-time members in 1967) needs in order to conduct its business: advisory (an elective executive committee), elementary composition, freshman literature, undergraduate advising, undergraduate study, undergraduate honors, graduate advising, graduate study, graduate examinations, fellowships and teaching associate selection, teacher preparation, library, prizes and contests, and one final committee on lectures, readings, occasions, and publicity. All committees except the advisory committee are appointed by the chairman, who also appoints ad hoc committees to deal with special problems. Standing committees range in size from five to ten members, and in 1966–67 they consumed the time of fifty-eight teachers (twenty-six of whom served on more than one committee). When one adds to these often onerous duties service on college or university-wide committees (to which, it sometimes seems, members of the English department are appointed with unusual frequency), it may appear that the primary threat to good teaching in American institutions of higher learning is not the demands of scholarship and publication but the heavy burden of committee work imposed on members of the faculty.

Assigning Courses and Planning the Curriculum. Decisions on who will teach what and thus, in many instances, on which courses will be offered are reached by committees in a few departments, but in most they are made by the chairman or his deputy after informal talks with individual members. In an overwhelming majority of cases (82 percent), the decisions are based on practical calculations of available competence rather than on some concept of the perfectly suitable program. That is, the chairman takes an inventory of the stock of competencies on hand and then determines which of his department's wares will be displayed; he does not first design an ideal curriculum and then deploy his staff accordingly. Or he may try to do both at once, in an effort to reconcile his supply of competence with the demands of the program he and his colleagues think most feasible and appropriate. When asked "What do you take most heavily into account as you plan and revise your course offerings for undergraduates?" 83.1 percent of all departments referred to the need to present a comprehensive set of courses. If—since 82 percent had referred to available competence—the figures seem contradictory, it is probably because the need fully to exploit the faculty's several talents often contradicts or conflicts with the need to offer a well-balanced curriculum. The chairman may have to find an assignment for his expert in modern poetry just when his program lacks a course in the literature of the eighteenth century. He would much prefer, of course, to have versatile teachers who could fill all the gaps in his curriculum (which accounts for the fact, previously noted, that a majority of departments now look for teachers of general ability when they recruit new members). Lacking such polymaths, he must somehow accommodate the department's resources to the students' needs, well aware that the compromise he contrives will probably not please everyone.

According to my findings on curriculum planning, most chairmen—when they turn to the annual agony of assigning their staff and designing a curriculum—pay some attention to individual preferences but very little to seniority or rank. Departments may indulge a few of their senior members who insist on teaching their favorite courses, but for practical as well as ethical reasons they usually decree that no one may "own" a course. Some go beyond this to ensure by various procedures that courses are regularly rotated or swapped: 24.8 percent of all departments rotate all courses, 12.4 percent rotate general but not special courses, 12.8 percent rotate at the request of the instructor, and 3.5 rotate because of scheduling conflicts. Because their complements of specialists are limited, many small departments find it difficult to rotate courses: the man who is fully qualified to teach linguistics must be asked to continue at that post, cannot be allowed to try his hand at teaching the modern novel. Larger departments can afford more mobility, both because they offer a greater variety of courses and because they have a larger stock of teaching competencies. Several of them—those at the University of California, Berkeley, at the University of North Carolina, and at San Francisco State College, for example—encourage their members to undertake the preparation and execution of new courses by redistributing some assignments each year.

Typical of those departments whose deployment of the manpower available to them permits the rotation of courses is that at the University of Connecticut. There almost all undergraduate classes in English are limited to thirty-five students (not, as we shall see, an unusually small number; the great majority of English classes taught in this country today consist of from ten to thirty students). Only two or three large lecture courses are offered each term; in all other courses, when enrollments increase, new sections are added. During a recent term fourteen of the department's fifty-eight members taught the basic course in Shakespeare, ten taught world literature in translation, and nine taught the modern novel. Enrollments were sufficient to justify four classes in American literature of the nineteenth century, three in Romantic literature, and four in the

English language (to cite but a few examples). All classes above the freshman level are taught by members of the regular staff, and each teacher proceeds independently, guided only by a loose "gentleman's agreement" on what the course should contain and should try to accomplish. These procedures result in a large supply of teaching assignments and allow each instructor to teach a variety of courses if he wishes. During the fall of 1971, one member taught world literature, early American literature, and Shakespeare. Another taught contemporary drama and the British novel. And a third somehow juggled literary criticism, the modern novel, and great narratives. Although most members of the department limit their teaching repertoires to three or four courses, opportunities to undertake new assignments are usually available.

The department which can offer such opportunities and can promise that all members will eventually be permitted to teach courses they covet enjoys an advantage in recruiting and retaining valuable young teachers. Chairmen of certain small departments in which courses have been preempted by senior members report that providing teaching assignments which will engage and satisfy their bright new Ph.D.s has become a major problem. "All I can give them is freshman English and the sophomore survey course, and that isn't enough," said the chairman of one department in Ohio. Furthermore, students as well as the department benefit when faculty members are allowed to teach those courses they can teach with maximum interest and enthusiasm. Rotation helps to prevent staleness, and it militates against the students' tendency to identify courses or subjects with the personalities of individual instructors ("Don't take Chaucer: the teacher's no good"). It improves morale not only because it is manifestly an equitable procedure but also because it ensures that department members will have teaching experiences in common, will be less likely to withdraw into their specialties. Some critics of rotation argue that it results in ill-informed, amateurish teaching; its advocates reply that most well-trained members of this profession are quite competent to prepare new courses appropriate to undergraduate instruction if they are given a year in which to do so. It may also be true that, as one old hand has said, "you teach best when you are most nervous, most aware of your own inadequacies."

Effecting Uniformity in Sectioned Courses. Should the course in Shakespeare, taught simultaneously by fourteen instructors, turn out a uniform product? Should the same texts be taught at the same pace in the same ways to communicate a specific body of knowledge and understanding which can be measured by a common examination? Some teachers, impressed by the uncertainty which attends all educational enterprises, think it impossible to achieve uniformity, either of instruction or of product; and they urge their departments simply to have faith in the teachers they have hired, leaving them to their own best devices. They are persuaded that freedom to teach according to one's own style and at one's own gait is more valuable than assurance that, no matter which section they have attended, all students have had the same course. Others are nagged by the realization that the entry "English 230" on a student's record may or may not mean that he has read *Richard II* or that he has acquired information about the conventions of the Elizabethan stage. Most multiclass courses are required in one way or another, and these teachers are inclined to agree with Albert R. Kitzhaber (1963) when he says (with dubious logic), "A required . . . course in a basic academic subject such as English ought to have a certain degree of uniformity from section to section; else it ought not to be required." They would not propose that teachers of sectioned courses march in lockstep, but they believe that all legitimate means to achieve uniformity should be tried. About 90 percent of those departments with sectioned courses subscribe to this view, and they use a variety of means, singly or in combination, to effect uniformity: staff meetings (68 percent); common syllabuses (61.9); common readings (61.5)—usually selected by committee (30.6 percent allow individual instructors to select their own texts for sectioned courses); common examinations (21.9); common lectures (12.2); common theme grading (1.2). If any or all of these practices result in fruitful collaboration and the improvement of courses, they may be justified, whether or not they succeed as devices to ensure uniformity. If, on the other hand, they stifle originality and discourage experimentation, they may be harmful to programs and disastrous for morale. In this, as in many other matters that affect many members of the department and large parts of its curriculum, much depends on how liberally and how tactfully regulations are administered.

Beneath this debate over departmental procedures lies a truly profound question, which arises in one version or another almost every time uniformity of teaching is discussed. It is the question of whether there can be—or ought to be—a right way to teach college English. This, in turn, raises the most disturbing question of all: Is English a discipline? Is it, as other disciplines claim to be, a systematic study of a limited body of evidence and interpretation? Or is it, as many would assert, a continuous *activity*, which leads to no certainty or conclusion and which is justified only as long as it enhances the aesthetic experience afforded by the materials it addresses? Those who believe that courses can be packaged tend to take the former position. Those who resist the regulation of teaching tend to take the latter. Many other debates which exercise the profession, from the running battle over freshman English to the continuing argument over requirements for the major, may also be seen as disputes between these rival concepts of English as an academic enterprise.

FOUR

Teaching Loads

As I have reported, only 10 per-
cent of all English departments are allowed to set their own teaching
loads; the rest must bargain with their deans and provosts to obtain
and maintain the lightest load which the needs and resources of the
institution will allow. It should be of great value to a department
engaged in such negotiations to be able to compare its lot with those
of other departments in institutions of similar or different sizes and
kinds in various parts of the nation. From the data I collected, it
was possible to define precisely how many departments of each size,
type, and geographical location labored under each load. Before
presenting these findings, however, I should acknowledge a distinction between teaching loads and total workloads. The former
means the number of class hours taught per week by a full-time
member of the department; the latter would include the many other
professional duties—preparing courses, correcting papers, counseling, and so forth—required of English teachers. Although it
might be possible to devise an elaborate formula for determining

total workloads, it would probably not be profitable to do so, because there are so many variations, not only among departments but also among individual teachers and their work habits, that such comparisons would have little meaning. The preamble to the "Statement on the Workload of the College Teacher," which the NCTE issued in 1965 and published in *College English* (October 1966), provides a useful review of most of the elements that compose the total workload.

In 1967 about 50 percent of all English departments at four-year colleges had a normal teaching load of twelve hours. This was by far the most common teaching load. The national percentages for all teaching loads were as follows: .7 percent of all departments had a six-hour load; 2.5 percent had a six-hour load one term and a nine-hour load the next; 16.4 percent had a nine-hour load; 10.4 percent had nine hours one term, twelve the next; 49.2 percent had twelve hours; 5.4 percent had twelve hours one term, fifteen the next; and 15 percent had fifteen hours. The NCTE's statement of policy on workloads declares that "a weekly teaching load of no more than nine hours should be considered the standard load for college teachers of English. And *under no circumstances* should any English teacher's weekly load exceed twelve hours." My figures reveal that in 1967, when colleges still enjoyed prosperity, 80 percent of all departments with four-year programs had teaching loads in excess of the NCTE's standards, and 20 percent had loads in excess of the maximum prescribed. One would expect to find a slightly higher incidence of heavy teaching loads today, when austerity has compelled a number of departments to reduce their staffs and to impose greater burdens on the surviving members.

Among departments of highest prestige (that is, those thought by members of the profession to offer unusually good programs for undergraduates), the most common teaching load was nine hours. This was the competitive figure which less fortunate departments sought to emulate. A few departments (for example, those at Amherst College and the University of Rochester) required only six hours of teaching from members at all ranks, but the tutorial load at most of these institutions was unusally high: instructors might be asked to meet for an hour a week with each of three or four honors students or others entitled to special privileges.

I also correlated teaching loads with class sizes to find out how many members of the profession teach how many students each term. Using the modal or most common class size rather than the average (which may be influenced by extreme, atypical cases), I discovered that the typical class size for a third of those who had nine-hour loads was from ten to nineteen students; for another third, twenty to thirty-nine students; and for 26 percent, thirty to forty-nine students. The most common class sizes for those who had twelve-hour loads were about the same, so that teachers in this group simply had one more class or about 25 percent more students (and perhaps one more course to prepare). Those who were so unfortunate as to teach fifteen hours a week usually had smaller classes, but their total student loads were higher. A very common combination was a teaching load of twelve hours and an enrollment mode of about thirty students per class. A teacher whose total assignment falls into this category is responsible for the instruction of about 120 students each term—too many, perhaps, to allow him to give proper attention to the needs of each.

Heavy teaching loads were more common in the southeastern and south central sections of the United States than in other sections: 31.4 percent of departments in the Southeast had fifteen hour loads, but only 5.1 percent of departments in the North Atlantic states had that load. On the other hand, 60.1 percent of departments in the North Atlantic region had twelve-hour loads as compared to 41.2 percent in the Southeast. Lower wages and heavier workloads have long put the schools in the south at a disadvantage in recruiting, though in today's buyers' market they seem to have no difficulty in attracting candidates.

In general, teaching loads varied in inverse proportion to the size of the school and the size of the department. That is, heavy teaching loads were more common in small schools than in large. Thus, 53.5 percent of departments with fewer than ten members had twelve-hour loads, 17.1 percent had fifteen-hour loads, whereas almost *all* departments with over seventy members had nine-hour loads. Heavy loads were also more common in departments that did not offer graduate programs than in those with graduate programs.

These and other figures on this subject are consistent with the implications of figures relating the size of school to the type of competency sought in candidates (whether specialized or general) and to criteria for tenure and promotion. When all these statistics are combined, they confirm one's impression that small schools are more likely than large to seek teachers of general ability, to value teaching over scholarly publication, and to expect their faculty members to teach long hours. In other words, emphasis on general ability increases as more teaching is demanded. Or one might say that the more teaching they require, the less expert knowledge departments can expect.

In 16.5 percent of all departments, there are no reduced loads; everyone teaches the full number of hours. Other departments reduce loads for the following reasons: chairman (58.2 percent of all departments); assistant chairman (7.2 percent); director of freshman English (12.9); director of graduate studies (9.3); other administrative duties (27.6); special nonteaching duties (26.9); special teaching assignments (13.3); research and publication (24); rank (2.5); seniority (.8); and other reasons (10.7). With the exception of the chairman, whose teaching load I have already discussed, members of the department who serve in the capacities listed are usually granted a reduction of three hours or one course. It is notable that very few departments award lighter teaching loads simply on the basis of seniority or rank and that almost a quarter of all departments reduce some members' loads in order to allow them more time for private research and publication. This practice is especially common among larger departments: about 85 percent of departments with over forty members grant such reductions. Relief of this kind is intended, like sabbatical leaves, to enable faculty members to pursue scholarly enterprises which will enrich their courses and enhance their department's prestige. Students and administrators on some campuses have complained, however, that the actual effect is to distract teachers from teaching, which further impoverishes already inadequate programs. They fear, and with some justice, that English teachers may seek to emulate their colleagues in the sciences, many of whom now devote most of their time to subsidized research rather than to teaching.

"Is this one of the terms you teach?" Professor Ephim Fogel

of Cornell says he was recently asked this charmingly naïve question by a neighbor who is a scientist. A single slip of this kind may seem to confirm the college English teacher's dark suspicion that he alone is laboring to sustain undergraduate education in America. Too often, however, his is *only* a paranoid suspicion: precisely how many hours per week each of his colleagues in other fields must spend in the classroom, he does not know. And how his total workload compares with theirs he can only guess. He has heard of foreign-language teachers who have twenty-hour loads and of scientists who must hold laboratory classes every afternoon. Finally, when pressed to decide whether his teaching load is equitable, he may grant that it probably is. Of all departments of English, 81 percent believe that, if their information is correct, their teaching loads compare favorably with those of other departments on their campuses. Some would argue that this statistic proves only that departments of English delude themselves. A thorough computation and comparison of workloads throughout the faculty would reveal, they say, that English teachers are required to work much harder than most. They would urge members of the profession to assert their rights and to insist on lighter loads commensurate with those of faculty members in other departments. This proposal, though certainly attractive to teachers of English, may fail to impress those administrators who have the authority to regulate teaching loads if it is not accompanied by a comprehensive review of the English department's function. How many hours the department is asked to teach is clearly dependent on what it is asked to accomplish—and, perhaps even more important, on what provinces and prerogatives it claims for itself. It may be overburdened because, in its greed, it has gathered to itself tasks which were best delegated to others.

FIVE

Department's
Responsibility
to the College

In one important respect the department of English is unique among the several faculties which serve at American colleges and universities: it alone has something all others must use. It is possible to practice many disciplines without using mathematics or the methods of the social sciences or the techniques of the sciences, but no discipline can be practiced without the use of English. As the college or university's principal authority on its common language, the English department inevitably claims or is delegated a kind of monopoly that is denied all other departments. Words are its stock in trade, and its goods are everywhere in demand. But the prosperity which accrues to the department because of the very nature of its subject often proves an embarrassment of riches which distracts the department from its goals, dissipates its energies, and greatly complicates its efforts to define its function. Because its specialty is not special but common, because its province is at once limited and general, the department cannot say, as others may, "Our function is to give students something which is new to them, which has intrinsic value, and which they can get only from us." Instead, it must concede that its services are often sought only as preparation for the practice of other disciplines or professions and that almost everything it has to offer is already in the common domain.

Until quite recently—say, within the past two decades— most departments of English proceeded blithely to exploit their singular monopoly and to expand their empires province by province. Undisturbed by the paradox that their wealth was largely a consequence of their having so little they could call their own, they gladly embraced almost every academic enterprise which could somehow be said to pertain to their discipline. The late William Riley Parker, who wrote the first critical history of the department of English as an institution, described its sudden growth late in the last century and its steady proliferation thereafter (1967, p. 348):

[English was] strongly affected by the educational events of the 1880s and 1890s. . . . This was a period in which the whole structure of higher education in America underwent profound changes, yielding to the pressures of new learning, the elective system, increased specialization, acceptance of the idea that practical or useful courses had a place in higher education, and, not least in importance, the actual doubling of college enrollments during the last quarter of the century. . . . It was in this atmosphere that "English" in the United States very recently became an accepted subject, grew to maturity, overreached itself, and planted deeply the seeds of most of its subsequent troubles as an academic discipline. Early chairmen and early professors of English literature were willing if not eager to increase the prestige of their subject and the numbers of their students and course offerings by embracing not only linguistics . . . but also rhetoric, which normally included, of course, oratory, elocution, and all forms of written composition.

It is well to remind ourselves, Parker says,

of the full scope of the aggressiveness (some would say acquisitiveness)
exhibited by departments of "English." They were later to embrace,
just as greedily, journalism, business writing, creative writing, writing
for engineers, playwriting, drama and theater, and American litera-
ture, and were eventually to be offering courses in contemporary
literature, comparative literature, the Bible and world classics in trans-
lation, American civilization, the humanities, and "English for foreign-
ers." In sum, English departments became the catchall for the work of
teachers of extremely diverse interests and training, united theoretically
but not actually by their common use of the mother tongue.

The history of the department of English, then, has been one of
aggrandizement, uneasy federation, and eventual dissolution. During
the first scramble for power it was presumed that almost any course
or program devoted to a study of the English language and its uses
was fit prey for the English department. Later it became apparent
that many of the subsidiaries English had seized were so specialized,
so diversified, and so popular in their own right that a common
concern for language was too dilute a bond to cement their federation. Thus, the department began to divest itself or to be relieved of
several of its functions. "Little by little," as Parker noted, "English
departments lost journalism, speech, and the theater, and recently
we have seen the development of separate undergraduate departments of comparative literature and linguistics. There have [even]
been polylingual grumblings from foreign-language departments
about the English department monopoly of courses in world literature" (1967, p. 350).

    Most departments have relinquished their adjunct programs
as gladly as they once appropriated them. The demand for their
courses in literature, which they rightly consider the core of their
curriculum, has continued to grow, and they are happy to con-
solidate their realm by surrendering provinces they probably should
never have acquired in the first place. Now, in the third quarter of
the century, it is still difficult to define "English" as a discipline,
but it is possible to delimit the department's domain and to approach
a reckoning of its responsibilities. This is best done by a process of
elimination—that is, by determining just how many departments

retain which peripheral functions and how many have abandoned them.

Adjunct Programs

Journalism. Courses in journalism are offered by 32.5 percent of the departments of English in four-year colleges and universities; over two thirds of all departments no longer feel obliged to provide such quasi-professional training. The number varies with the size of the department and the size of the institution. Departments of medium size—say, from ten to twenty members— are most likely to retain their courses in journalism, probably because they cannot ignore the demand for such courses and there is no one else to teach them. Few small departments can afford to offer these courses, and at most large institutions journalism is now taught by a separate faculty.

Speech. An even smaller number of departments of English continue to provide courses in speech. Parker (1967, p. 340) reminds us that "English was born about 100 years ago [and] its mother . . . was oratory—or what we now prefer to call public speaking or, simply, speech." Now over 70 percent of all English departments have disengaged themselves from their parent discipline. Only 28.9 percent offer courses in speech, and the number is higher (about 40 percent) among small departments than among large (only about 10 percent). The recent revival of the study of rhetoric in courses in written composition might suggest that a rapprochement of English and oratory may soon be effected; certain texts (for example, the speeches of Adlai Stevenson and Martin Luther King, Jr.) and the commentaries of certain critics (notably Kenneth Burke) are now the common property of both speech and English courses. And if Marshall McLuhan's analysis of "the movement away from book culture toward oral communication" has any validity, it will surely become necessary for English teachers to devote more and more attention to the spoken word. At present, however, the gap between the departments of English and speech seems to be widening, and neither manifests much inclination to bridge it.

Theater and Dramatics. Though almost all English departments teach dramatic literature, only a very few—3.6 percent of the total—now offer courses in acting or the techniques of the theater. On many campuses those who are competent to conduct such courses have joined those who teach public speaking in a separate department of speech and drama. Collaboration between that faculty and the department of English may have great benefits for both: English teachers are properly embarrassed by the realization that the plays they discuss with their students were not written to be apprehended from the page, and they welcome opportunities to share performances with their students. Too often, however, the dissociation of dramatics and English in the organizational structure of the institution results in rivalry and backbiting as both compete to assert their rights to represent the playwrights.

Technical and Business Writing. Of all departments, 32.9 percent teach technical (and/or scientific) writing, and 10.9 percent offer instruction in writing business correspondence and reports. These are frankly identified as service courses, designed to prepare students to communicate effectively in the worlds of technology, science, and commerce. They are devoted entirely to the analysis and composition of what is called (with unfortunate imprecision) "expository prose," and the values they foster are almost exclusively those of the professions they serve. Members of the department who teach in these programs are often an embattled band who see themselves slighted and their courses depreciated by their literary colleagues. Fred H. Macintosh, Director of Advanced Composition at the University of North Carolina, Chapel Hill, expressed typical pique when he defined the problems which beset his enterprise: "increasing enrollments; virtually no trained people to staff growing programs; no programs to train teachers for these courses; almost no English teachers with writing experience outside the academic world (and very few with realistic notions of the writing situations and criteria outside academe); control of these courses by chairmen who have long thought primarily in terms of literature courses, literary scholarship, and English majors preparing to teach literature." It is not surprising, therefore, that some teachers of technical and business writing who feel neglected have seceded from the department of English to establish separate programs under the auspices of schools of engineering, science, and business administration.

English as a Second Language. Years ago it was rumored that, because no special provision was made for their instruction, most foreign students at Harvard were automatically awarded a "Chinese C" when they took courses in English. No such polite evasion is now necessary. Within the past twenty years a new pedagogy, informed with the insights of modern linguistics, has developed to meet the specific needs of students who come to this country inadequately prepared to cope with studies conducted in English. Courses in English as a second language are now offered to both undergraduate and graduate students at many institutions that annually attract appreciable numbers of foreigners. At least three diagnostic examinations have been devised to identify those who need help, and specially trained teachers make every effort to correct "faults" of oral and written expression, many of which may be attributed to differences which linguists can detect between the student's native language and English. Although the demand for these courses will probably never be very large on any one campus, because the number of foreign students attending most American colleges and universities is not large, English as a second language has already emerged as a new profession, adjunct to English but separate from it in purpose and methods.

Here, then, is a small but impeccable enterprise which English departments might be expected jealously to embrace if they were determined to preserve or to enlarge their empires. At present, however, only 20 percent of all English departments offer courses in English as a second language, and on several campuses this new province has already been annexed by other departments— with the full consent and approval of the department of English. Where there are separate departments of linguistics (as at the University of Michigan and the University of Connecticut), English as a second language has usually been assigned to them; elsewhere it is taught by members of the department of foreign languages or by a separate staff. In this instance as in others, the English department has displayed none of its old rapacity and has freely acknowledged the ability of others to perform teaching tasks it might once have reserved for itself.

Of all English departments 18.9 percent have no adjunct programs, provide no special service courses. Among the 81 percent that do, the majority devote less than 10 percent of their total teaching effort to such ancillary offerings. For most departments, then, the auxiliary programs that the profession preempted early in this century do not now constitute a very large commitment. Those who conduct these programs form a small (and often disgruntled) minority within the department, and persuading new members of the profession to teach such courses is proving more and more difficult. Certainly the general trend is toward decentralization and delegation, toward retrenchment within the department, toward consolidating its curriculum and relinquishing functions and power it once coveted. As a result, many English departments now retain only one service obligation—but that is the largest and most vexatious of all.

SIX

Freshman English

"Surprising as the idea may first appear to you," writes Parker (1967, p. 347), "there was, of course, no compelling reason at the outset why the teaching of *composition* should have been entrusted to teachers of the English language and literature." It was, he says, almost by historical accident that composition was originally consigned to the English department.

To sum up: the ancient subject of rhetoric, which at first showed signs of adapting itself to changing times while preserving both its integrity and its vitality, in the nineteenth century lost both integrity and independent vitality by dispersing itself to academic thinness. It permitted oratory to become identified with elocution, and, as for written composition, it allowed this to become chiefly identified with that dismal, unflowering desert, freshman theme writing. It is little wonder that speech and composition were readily accepted by administrators as appendices of English literature.

Over 70 percent of all departments of English have since relinquished their claim to the first of these appendices, but English,

62

as Parker notes, "has somehow managed to hold on stubbornly to all written composition not intended for oral delivery—a subject which has always had a most tenuous connection with the academic study of language and literature, but which, not incidentally, from the outset has been a great secret strength for 'English' with both administrators and public, and latterly has made possible the frugal subsidizing of countless graduate students who cannot wait to escape it." What was acquired by default has become the largest single component of the American college and university curriculum and a program so crucial to the welfare of English departments that it conditions most of what they do.

Magnitude

In fall 1967, four-year colleges and universities in the United States enrolled 1,338,474 freshmen. Of these institutions, 93.2 percent required at least one term of English. Even if 20 percent of all entering students were granted exemption (and the actual figure was probably smaller than that), the number enrolled in freshman English was well over one million. About 75 percent of these students were required to take a second term as well, so that the total number of credits awarded for freshman English (or the total number of hours students spent in freshman classes) during the full year was about five and one half million. The number of papers written and corrected may well have exceeded fifteen million—a figure to send the mind reeling!

Although only 31.3 percent of all undergraduates were freshmen and not all freshmen took English, departments of English devoted *over 40 percent* of their total teaching effort to this gigantic educational enterprise. (For reasons difficult to divine, this figure varied in direct proportion to the size of the school: it was 37.8 percent for small schools, 42.5 percent for medium-sized, and 44.8 percent for large.) The principal reason for the discrepancy between the amount of teaching devoted to freshmen and the number of freshmen is that many students take no English after their first year, and therefore most of the department's clientele are freshmen. Furthermore, freshman English is especially costly of teaching manpower and time: the number of students taught in each class is small, and the number of papers to be read is large. It is ironic that the course or program which serves the largest mass of students is one of those least amenable to mass instruction. The result is that freshman English makes enormous demands on the department. How well those demands are met proves a good index of the department's general health.

Staffing Freshman English

The most populous course in the English department's curriculum is usually the least popular with its members, principally because teaching freshman English entails great amounts of repetitive work. A course in composition inevitably produces compositions, and these must be read. The prospect of correcting piles of freshman themes and of discussing elementary topics with beginning students prompts many instructors, especially those of senior rank, to avoid participation in the freshman program. Many others recognize, however, that this arduous assignment has its own rewards; that most freshmen *are* fresh, responsive, and a pleasure to teach; and that, precisely because they are fundamental, the questions one must raise in freshman classes are among the most difficult and the most intriguing any professional student of language and literature may address. Certainly it is clear that unless the department persuades a sufficient number of its best teachers to accept this assignment, its freshman program becomes a kind of ghetto, slighted by students and staff alike.

My survey disclosed that in 1967 all members of the department taught freshman English in 44.2 percent of all schools; that percentage is probably larger in 1973 because the general decline in enrollments in upper-division English courses has forced even senior professors to return to teaching freshmen. That figure was significantly higher for private schools (57.4 percent) than for public schools (33 percent), with sectarian schools falling in between. The chairman (and he alone) is exempted from teaching freshmen at 10.8 percent of all schools, specialists are exempted at 7.5 percent, graduate faculty members at 3.6; and those whose schedules and workloads preclude at 12.2. At 19.4 percent of all institutions, freshmen are taught by the regular staff and graduate students; at only 1.8 percent, they are taught by graduate students alone. In short, the responsibility for educating freshmen is shared by all or most members in a majority of departments. But that does not mean that a majority of American freshmen are taught by experienced, full-time teachers of English, because the percentage of departments in which all members teach freshmen is much higher among small private schools than among the large public schools that most American college students attend. Furthermore, the percentage of public schools employing graduate students to teach their freshman courses is appreciably greater than the percentage of private institutions. It follows, of course, that the student who is admitted to a private college or university (and who can afford to attend) enjoys a much better chance of studying English with an experienced (and properly paid) instructor than his opposite number at the state college or university does. This may be the only qualitative difference between the brands of freshman English offered at private and at public institutions. In most other respects—size of classes, content of courses, texts used, and number of papers assigned—freshman English programs are now much alike at public, private, and sectarian schools; or those differences which do occur are not attributable to differences in types of institutions. But the freshman who enters a small private college (at an extra cost to his parents of about $2500 a year) will probably be taught by a man who also teaches seniors majoring in English, whereas his high school classmate who enters a large state university will probably be taught by a graduate student who was himself a senior majoring in English only a few years before.

It is quite possible, however, that the freshman who studies with a graduate teaching assistant will find his English classes more stimulating than will the student who works with a senior member of the department. The teaching abilities of graduate students probably vary just about as those of full-time members of the profession do: some are imaginative and well informed, others are dull. But all enjoy a special advantage because of the proximity of their age to their students' and because of their fresh enthusiasm for teaching. In this sense they and their freshman are well matched. The fact remains, however, that the graduate student *does* lack experience, both as a teacher and as a scholar-critic. And because he lacks experience, he lacks versatility; his repertoire is limited; and often he must teach out of poverty of knowledge and insight.

Departments which conduct graduate programs should—indeed, must—provide such apprenticeships; but, as the Allen report suggests, they "should regard [the graduate student's] teaching as part of [his] education, not as a means of staffing courses."

Although only about 20 percent of *all* departments employ graduate students to teach freshman courses, a majority of departments at large public institutions (which educate most American undergraduates) do so. In departments with graduate programs, the average ratio of full-time teachers to graduate students on the freshman English staff is 1:1; that is, about half the members of the staff are teachers of some experience, and about half are apprentices. (It should be added that the graduate students often teach more freshman sections than the regular members of the staff.) At several very large universities, however, no such nice balance is maintained: at Kansas State University the ratio is 1:4, at Purdue it is 1:5, at UCLA 1:10, and at the University of Illinois (Champaign-Urbana) 1:30. Such overdependence on—or exploitation of—teaching assistants may have unfortunate consequences at both ends of the department's curriculum: its freshman program comes to rely on its graduate program for inexpensive manpower, and its graduate program is subsidized to a large degree by its freshman program. Neither program benefits from this unhealthy relationship; in a certain sense each preys on the other.

A number of departments have recently taken steps to eliminate this excessive interdependence. An example is that at the University of Pennsylvania, where almost all of freshman English was taught by graduate students until 1966. Since then the department has made a number of four-year fellowships available to candidates for the Ph.D. These subsidies call for only one year of service as an "apprentice-teacher" (serving as an assistant to a full-time member of the staff) and one year as a teaching assistant (during which the graduate student conducts one section of freshman English). The plan requires inducing many members of the regular staff to return to teaching freshmen, and this has been achieved in part by revising the freshman program to convert courses in composition to courses in literature and composition; eventually at least 50 percent of Pennsylvania's freshmen will be taught by experienced faculty members. This is a costly solution, but any bold attack on such a large problem must entail expense. Even if the department's freshman program is reduced in size or eliminated entirely (possibilities soon to be discussed), the need to support its graduate students will remain.

Remedial English

In 1960 a survey conducted by the NCTE found that 55.6 percent of all four-year colleges and universities provided special remedial instruction for students who were "deficient in their use of English." By 1967 that number had decreased dramatically: only 27 percent, or less than half the previous number, continued to offer remedial English. This means that within seven years over one quarter of all departments felt they could justly abandon their courses for inadequately trained freshmen. A counterwave or reversal of this trend has since occurred as more and more institutions have actively recruited or have offered open admission to disadvantaged students. An example is Dartmouth, which, in 1969, for the first time in its history, hired an instructor specifically to teach remedial English. His classes are composed largely of black students, who now constitute 10 percent of Dartmouth's freshman class. Even in 1967 some 470 departments (many of them in large public institutions, where remedial English is most common) evidently believed they must continue to expend part of their (probably inadequate) resources on these subcollegiate college courses.

Possibly because such courses are still offered throughout the University of California system, remedial English is much more common in the West than in other parts of the nation. Several of the public institutions that have retained their remedial programs are located in states where, as Albert Kitzhaber (1963, p. 18) puts it, "legal requirements prevent selective admission." One of these is Nevada. There are few junior colleges in that state, and the university is compelled by law to admit every graduate of a Nevada high school who wishes to attend. About 10 percent of those admitted are "unable in placement examinations to demonstrate the proficiency in expression normally expected of high school graduates" (to quote the English department's manual for freshmen) and are assigned to English A, a remedial course that "affords extensive practice in elementary composition, together with a review of the fundamentals of English grammar and usage." This describes the typical remedial course and the procedures used to identify those students who need it. The course usually consists of little more than elementary drill in the mechanics of language. Three weeks may be devoted to the predicate, another two to basic punctuation, and so forth. Textbooks are primers of the kind used in some junior high schools. And, as Kitzhaber (1963, p. 19) notes, "The papers [assigned] are nearly always short—no more than a page or two—and often may consist of only a single paragraph. . . . A large proportion of the writing is done in class, sometimes all of it." There can be little intellectual substance in these courses, which the students aptly call "bonehead English."

Some colleges and universities assign students to remedial English if their high school grades in English were unusually low; others rely on their own placement examinations; most use nationally administered tests of verbal aptitude. At about 10 percent of all the schools that offer it, remedial English is conducted as a "clinic" or tutorial service to which students are remanded by faculty members or to which they repair voluntarily. Where classes are held, they are usually small (the enrollment mode is about eighteen students), and individual conferences are frequent.

Sixty-two percent of the schools that offer remedial courses award no credit for them; 14 percent charge an extra fee. Some students who are consigned to this limbo therefore suffer a double penalty: they are given retarded (as opposed to advanced) placement, and they must pay for it. It is no wonder that their discontent equals that of their teachers.

Very few faculty members want to teach remedial English, and most departments hope to eliminate it as soon as possible. That so many have already done so can probably be attributed to (1) the "pressure of rising enrollments and . . . [the] national concern for raising educational standards at all levels" which Kitzhaber noted in 1963 (p. 18); (2) the rapid growth of the junior and community colleges, which now provide suitable instruction for some of the students English departments in four-year institutions would have placed in remedial courses; and (3) widespread skepticism about the efficacy of remedial programs. There is reason to doubt that any course of instruction, no matter how carefully designed and compassionately taught, can "remedy" the verbal faults committed by eighteen-year-old students who cannot cope with the regular freshman program; institutions like the University of Nevada report that less than 5 percent of those students who begin with remedial English ever graduate.

The NCTE report of 1960 estimated that about five million dollars was being spent annually on salaries of teachers of remedial English in four-year colleges and universities. While the number of departments offering such programs decreased steadily during the late sixties, salaries increased by about a third from the $5000 mean the NCTE's study assumed, so the cost of remedial English must have remained almost constant. Now it has risen again. Instruction of this kind is, of course, essential to such daring experiments as the open-admissions plan at the City Universities of New York, but its high cost and low yield cannot be denied.

Requirements and Exemptions

The tradition that all undergraduates should begin their college careers with a course in English remains well established. Of all four-year colleges and universities in the nation, 93.2 percent require freshmen to take at least one term of English, 77.8 percent require them to take two, and 10 percent (almost all of which have the trimester or quarter-type calendar) require three. (These figures also reveal, of course, that only 15.4 percent of all institutions require only one term of freshman English and that the great majority require a full year.) There are signs, however, which suggest that the assumption, so generally held throughout the first half of the century, that no college student should graduate without having had at least one course in English is now being questioned. A number of leading colleges and universities—Amherst, Yale, Northwestern, and the University of Colorado, for example—have recently abandoned their freshman English requirements (though not their English courses for freshmen), and at least one new institution, the University of California at Santa Cruz, has no freshman program to require. A survey conducted by the MLA in 1971 (and reported in the May 1971 *ADE Bulletin*) found that 38 percent of the departments polled had reduced or eliminated their freshman requirements and that another 14 percent planned to do so within two

years; 49 percent of four-year institutions had either reduced or
eliminated their all-college English requirements. English departments on other campuses are asking their colleagues in other fields
to review their motives for insisting that all students take English
and to entertain the possibility that this requirement should be
liberalized or eliminated. They point out that high school instruction in English is gradually improving; that students arrive at college
today somewhat better trained in the arts of composition than those
who enrolled as freshmen, when the present requirements were
established; and that the uses and conventions of English in the
several disciplines are becoming so diverse that no one course in
English can possibly meet all the needs of all departments. Even
at those institutions where the department's efforts to encourage a
new and more realistic view of freshman requirements have met
with success, however, they have not always resulted in greatly
lightening its freshman load: at some of the institutions mentioned
above which have eliminated their requirements, over 80 percent of
all freshmen continue to elect courses in English.

A majority of four-year colleges and universities—58.8
percent—grant exemptions from their freshman English requirements to students of unusual ability. Large public institutions, which
have more heterogeneous student bodies and a greater variety of
freshman courses, are more likely than medium-sized or small to
grant exemptions. Exemptions are most commonly awarded for
superior performance on nationally administered examinations: 30
percent of all institutions use such tests as the College Board's
Scholastic Aptitude Test—Verbal and the Co-operative English
Test to identify those students who will be excused from all or part
of their freshman English programs. At a growing number of institutions students are granted exemption if they perform well enough
on the Educational Testing Service's College Level Examination
Program (CLEP) Examination. Another 22.1 percent use their
own placement examinations; 10.5 percent consider the student's
high school record and his class standing; 7.5 percent have freshman classes for honors students, who are exempted from the regular
program (and who may be selected by one or several of the previous
methods); 22.8 percent use such means and evidence as personal
interviews, instructors' recommendations, and even samples of stu-

dents' handwriting. At several schools students are exempted from a second freshman course if they perform well enough in the first.

Specific criteria for exemption vary greatly, even among institutions that use the same national examinations. At the University of North Carolina students are exempted from the basic course in composition if their SAT-V scores are 600 or above, at the University of Oregon the cutoff point is 650, and at the University of Virginia it is 675. A number of schools at which the mean SAT-V score for the freshman class is high (say, about 630) grant no exemptions at all; the list includes Stanford, Grinnell, Wheaton College (Mass.), and the University of California, Berkeley. Many policies on exemption are quite arbitrary, or if there is a reason for them it is merely that the department of English is attempting to control the size of its freshman classes by excusing a sufficient number of students. Other policies express a judicious estimate of the actual abilities signified by the scores and of the educational value the courses will have for students of different abilities. Some departments are willing to acknowledge that their basic courses will probably have little value for students of unusual ability, and they have no desire to prevent students from proceeding as rapidy as possible. Other departments are confident that their freshman courses are so rich and challenging that they are justified in requiring all students to take them. In general, departments in the latter group are found at institutions of high prestige, which can be highly selective in admissions. At such schools (many of which are small and private) freshman English has become, not a service course, but the best introduction to the world of letters the English department can contrive, an introduction they believe all students need.

Advanced Placement

In 1954 the College Entrance Examination Board inaugurated its Advanced Placement Program "to provide a practical way for schools and colleges to create and use common definitions of college-level courses which, when completed in secondary school, prepare students for advanced study at college." It now provides course descriptions and conducts special examinations in eleven subject-matter areas, one of which is English. In each field the Board convenes a panel of specialists from the schools and colleges, who compose a general description of an ideal freshman course (or revise a previous description) to be taught to high school seniors of unusual ability and an examination designed to determine whether they have achieved college-level competence in the subject. The courses are taught by members of the high school staff and are usually considered a choice teaching assignment. The students form a small elite, far superior in academic ability to the average American college freshman.

The course in English currently recommended by the Advanced Placement Examining Committee is of a familiar type: it combines training in "practical criticism" or the close reading of literary texts with frequent writing assignments. Its purpose is "to teach the intelligent, mature student how to read works of literature and how to express himself about them." It is not a course in composition or rhetoric as such, although it assumes that students will acquire proficiency in those arts as they compose their responses to literary works. The list of works suggested as appropriate (but not mandatory) reads much like a description of the typical fare of the standard freshman "Introduction to Literature": it runs from *Hamlet* to *Death of a Salesman,* from *Pride and Prejudice* to *All the King's Men,* and from Wyatt to Lowell. There are few surprises and very little contemporary literature.

The examination, which is administered nationally and which all students who wish to apply for advanced placement under the College Board's plan must take, lasts three hours. It consists of a short objective section (multiple-choice questions on a poem or passage of prose), and three or four essay questions. In recent years the latter, which form the bulk of the examination, have included questions on an unidentified poem, questions on an unidentified prose passage, and a general question intended to enable students to demonstrate their understanding of two or three works they have read in the course. The objective test is scored electronically; answers to the essay questions are judged by a committee of readers, who award a composite grade based on the entire examination. Grades run from 1 to 5 and are explained as follows: "1—no recommendation, 2—possibly qualified [for advanced placement], 3—qualified, 4—well qualified, 5—extremely well qualified." In midsummer the student's answers to the essay questions (but not his record on the objective test) are sent to the college he will enter in the fall. With the examination booklet is sent the score the college board readers have given him (and, in many cases, a statement from his high school, describing the course he took, the grade he received, and the opinion of his teacher or principal). The college is free to make its own evaluation of the student's answers, of course, and it may or may not agree with the board's judgment. (If there is disagreement, it may be because the college has not been shown the student's score on the objective test.) The college then decides whether the student will be granted advanced placement and on what terms.

At most colleges and universities the number of entering students who have taken the College Board course and examination and who sue for advanced placement is very small: the average is less than 1 percent of the entering class. But these are excellent students who deserve special consideration, and for this reason alone most colleges try to formulate policies on advanced placement which will enable students to enter courses appropriate to their attainments. Any of several policies may be adopted. The College Board suggests that "participating colleges will normally wish to grant advanced placement or credit, or both, to candidates who receive grades of 3 or higher and will wish to review the examinations of those students who receive a grade of 2."

When asked to describe their policies on advanced placement, 29 percent of the departments in my sample reported that they grant exemption and/or credit to students receiving a grade of 3 or higher; 12.2 percent grant exemption for some higher (or lower) score; and 13.3 percent follow some other procedure. Among those who participate in the Board's program just about half grant course credits (which may be used to fulfill requirements for graduation, thus enabling the student to accelerate); the other half grant only exemption or have no fixed policy. Of all departments, however, 39.2 percent said that they award neither exemption nor credit for college work done in high school under the College Board's plan. If this figure is reliable, it means that over a third of all colleges and universities in the land do not acknowledge the board's program or make no provision for rewarding students who have participated in it.

Which of these policies have been adopted by the relatively

few institutions that regularly attract large numbers of advanced-placement students? The College Board reports that, in 1968, 30.7 percent of all students who took its examination in English subsequently matriculated at forty-one institutions, each of which enrolled over ninety advanced-placement candidates. Analysis of the policies of these institutions reveals that 58.5 percent grant exemption for grades of 3 and above, 34 percent accept only grades of 4 and 5, 4.8 percent accept grades of 2 and above, and only one school in the group has no fixed policy on advanced placement. (No information on how many award credit is available.) Some of these institutions actively recruit advanced-placement students, just as they recruit National Merit Scholars.

Not all college teachers of English, however, endorse the College Board's program. Many who are directly concerned with freshman programs express the following misgivings and complaints:

1. That the Advanced Placement Examination in English is a very imperfect instrument. The objective section is of slight value and may even be invalid, as the Graduate Record Examination probably is; fortunately this part counts for little. The essay questions do not test the student's ability to compose coherent expressions of well-deliberated thought and opinion, and it is this ability that many freshman courses—particularly those devoted to rhetoric and the study of nonliterary prose—are designed to foster. Departments offering such courses say, then, that they cannot use the Advanced Placement Examination as a means of identifying students who should be exempted from their freshman programs. Naturally they also wish that more attention were paid to the arts of composition and rhetoric in the advanced-placement course the College Board recommends.

Even those departments whose freshman courses closely resemble the Board's frequently express dissatisfaction with its examination. They complain of questions which seem to dictate responses and of questions which are so general as to invite rehashes of critical cliches. They say they find, as they read the examination booklets which are sent to them, that too often the students' answers to the essay questions offer no clear indication of whether they have acquired the reading habits the departments want their sophomores to have.

2. That sixteen-year-old students are not sufficiently mature to fully comprehend the works of literature read in advanced placement courses. "Sure, they can decipher *The Waste Land* or almost any other work you ask them to read," said one instructor, "but I doubt that they can *understand* the poem, because they haven't lived long enough to share experiences with the poet. Advanced placement and acceleration breed little monsters, premature sophisticates who can drop names but do little more." This charge overlooks the fact that even if students do not read *The Waste Land* in high school they may read it only nine months later in college, all the while they are happily assimilating films, novels, folk songs, and other products of the imagination which assume that they can understand matters just as profound as "fear in a handful of dust." There is no doubt, however, that it takes a skillful and imaginative teacher to render demanding works of literature—particularly works from the remote past—intelligible and amenable to adolescents. And this leads to the most serious criticism of the Advanced Placement Program, one which college teachers are reluctant to make but which they often express among themselves.

3. That too many high school teachers to whom the advanced-placement course is consigned are incompetent to teach it. From students' answers to the essay questions—especially those that ask them to comment on works they have read under instruction—college authorities can only infer that the level of discussion in many high school advanced-placement courses is lamentably low. Too often students offer mere synopsis for critical analysis (despite specific injunctions on the examination); too often their interpretations are stale, superficial, and oversimple. To read a set of replies to almost any one of the general questions is to pass through yards of standard prose about "Macbeth as a tragic figure" and "Willy Loman as a symbol of our times"; there is little evidence of original thought or personal insight. The suspicion arises that many advanced-placement students have been supplied "official" readings of the suggested works by teachers who received them from somewhere else. That the teachers are capable of reading the works

as the colleges expect their students to read them—that is, with attention to verbal texture, structure, and complexities of meaning—sometimes seems doubtful.

A few colleges and universities have not been content merely to criticize the Advanced Placement Program and the teachers who conduct it in the high schools but have sought to improve it to the benefit of their own undergraduate programs. Thus, the English department at the University of Oregon, with the support of the Ford Foundation, has worked to encourage high schools in its state to institute advanced-placement courses and has collaborated with teachers in the schools to ensure that those courses meet college standards. Members of the department report that this effort has already brought better-trained students to their campus. The promise of the Advanced Placement Program is that it affords opportunities of this kind to weld the seam between school and college and to offer good students rich courses at a time when they are best prepared to learn.

Varieties of Freshman English

In two respects the freshman courses at Carleton College, the University of Washington, and Dillard University, to name three disparate schools, are alike: at all these institutions—and most others—classes are small and students are required to write frequent papers. In almost every other respect they differ. The "enormous variety" which Kitzhaber found when he surveyed freshman English in 1961 is still apparent, and it does not seem that any single concept of the course or any one policy on freshman English will soon prevail. The ideal program which teachers and administrators (and textbook publishers) have sought for fifty years has not yet emerged, and the debate over freshman English continues much as before. When that debate is conducted by men who have pondered the ultimate implications of their arguments, however, it leads to matters fundamental to the concerns of all English departments; just as the freshman course is basic, so are the problems it raises. To rehearse the debate and to review the varieties of freshman English now offered is therefore to anatomize much of the profession's most significant thought and practice.

About one matter there seems to be little argument: it is

generally agreed that, whatever is taught or done in freshman
English, the course should provide abundant opportunities for
discussion and for direct communication between the student and
his teacher. Despite steadily increasing enrollments, most colleges
and universities have managed to keep their freshman English
classes small: the most common size is about twenty-five students.
Some have incorporated one or even two lecture meetings a week,
but almost all retain at least one class in which students are encouraged to share their thoughts with their teachers and their fellow
students. At many large universities his English class may offer the
freshman his only opportunity to participate in the free exchange of
ideas and to confer with a professional intellectual. This may be the
best reason for limiting the size of freshman English classes and,
indeed, the chief justification of freshman English itself. Dudley
Bailey, until recently chairman of English at the University of
Nebraska, writes (1968, p. 12):

*I have never heard an argument for increasing the [teaching] load at
the freshman level—except that it is a way of reducing professorial
loads. The usual arguments against it are those about the importance of
composition and the paper load; I find these arguments a lot of
malarkey, and I think many other chairmen do also. But I should
oppose increase in the size of freshman classes on other grounds: it is
probably wrong to place the heaviest teaching load on the youngest
staff, however we may rationalize doing so with talk of limber bones
and all that; and it is certainly wrong to place beginning students in
the largest classes. The central problem of the modern university of
some size is giving to the incoming student the sense that he is joining
an intellectual community, of a size that he can understand and deal
with. I find it rather droll to talk to anybody about an intellectual
community of 20,000 or 40,000; none of us really adjusts to a community a tenth that size. It seems to me ridiculous to talk of such a
community to the freshman student; I am not surprised that in most
cases the student identifies with a community which can hardly be
called an inellectual one—not everybody associated with a large university is as stupid as the faculty. We ought to have sense enough to
realize that if the student is ever to cope with the modern megalo-
versity, he must somewhere catch hold of it; and I doubt that he will
succeed unless we can start him off in small and hopefully comfortable
groups.*

This cogent argument implies that freshman English may serve, better than any other course taken during the first year in college, as something students may "catch hold of" and as an introduction to the intellectual life. Despite the variety, the confusion, and the imperfections of freshman English as it is taught today, it frequently does just that. As Robert Gorell (1965, p. 92) has written, "Students often testify, as they look back, that their freshman English course first brought their minds to life. . . . Because freshman English classes are still relatively small in most institutions, the instructor is often able to provide individual help for the student; he often becomes a counselor as well as a teacher, just because he is less remote than the lecturer in the large introductory courses. Often students even learn to write better."

If they do so, it may be because they have never before been asked to write so much under such close supervision. Of all departments 40.2 percent require freshmen to write eleven to fifteen papers a term, or about a theme a week; another 23.6 percent require nine or ten. Only 16.5 percent require fewer than seven papers a term (and only 3.5 percent more than fifteen). A long paper (usually, but not always, a "research" paper) is assigned by 43.3 percent. Most freshmen, then, must write about five thousand words for their English teachers during their first term at college. (At many institutions fewer papers are required during the second term.) The 125 million words (give or take a few million) they produce each year are invited—indeed, demanded—by teachers who can take little joy in reading most of them but who can see no way to work with students on their use of language other than by asking them to use it. Very few teachers now delude themselves that they can improve their students' ability to write simply by requiring them to write more often; but most find that to accomplish the purposes of the courses they have conceived they must confront students with a variety of writing tasks. In short, the good teacher of freshman English never asks for sheer quantity of prose, but he often finds himself reading quantites of themes because he believes the aims of his course demand them.

It is when they turn to defining those aims and to deciding what freshman English is all about that those who teach it begin to diverge. The principal question that divides them is whether their freshman courses should be conceived as service courses (designed to provide general training in verbal skills) or as "English" courses (designed to prepare students for further work in that field). About half the departments in the nation—48.9 percent, to be exact—still believe that freshman English should serve the community as a whole by instructing students in techniques of composition they may use whenever they are called upon to write. Of the remaining half, a few (6.9 percent) have abandoned this concept entirely and now see their freshman courses solely as introductions to the study of English at the college level. The rest try to pursue both goals, either simultaneously or in separate terms. In other words, English departments in the United States are about evenly divided between those that offer the freshman utilitarian training and those that offer him something more. The distinction is roughly, but not exactly, that which Kitzhaber (1963, pp. 2, 3) made between the "practical" view of freshman English, according to which "the course exists to provide immediate therapy for students whose academic future is clouded by their inability to manage the written form of English," and the "liberal" view, which "assumes that the primary purpose of the course is to focus the student's attention on fundamental principles of clear thinking and the clear and effective expression of that thinking." Many teachers and departments, inspired by a new sense of the integrity of their discipline, would now expand Kitzhaber's "liberal" view, enlarging it to include some reference to literary values and the humanizing effect of literary studies. With one chairman they would declare their "growing unwillingness to exist as a 'service department' for the rest of the university" and assert their desire "to devote [their] interests and utilize [their] specializations in those areas for which [the department] exists, viz., literary art and humanistic thought." These departments see theirs as a choice not between "therapy" and a course in "clear thinking" but between exercising and educating, between coaching students for future occasions which may demand the use of language and confronting them with present occasions which require the use of all their mental faculties.

Related to this distinction between rival concepts of freshman English and its purpose is a radical distinction between theories of composition and how it should be taught. "When someone teaches composition," Kitzhaber (1963, p. 89) justly observes, "he is trying to cultivate in the student a bafflingly complex intellectual skill." Just what is involved in the practice of that skill no one really knows. A 1963 summary, "The State of Knowledge about Composition," concludes with a section entitled "Unexplored Territory," which lists some twenty-four questions which have yet to be answered; the last of these is the simple but all-embracing query "Of what does skill in writing really consist?" (Braddock, 1963, p. 53). Unable to define the skill they would impart, much less to engender it at will, teachers of composition fashion courses which they hope, more or less blindly, will encourage the writing habits they prefer. In doing so they commit themselves, wittingly or otherwise, to certain unprovable assumptions about the nature of the writing process. Louis Milic (1965, p. 142) has helped them define those assumptions and their pedagogical consequences by identifying (with some oversimplification) the theories of style available to teachers of composition.

There are only three real theories of style, though there has been much embroidery on the basic fabric. The most familiar is the theory of ornate form, or rhetorical dualism. From the classical rhetoricians who originated it to the rhetoricians of the moment who are still using it, this dualism view has always implied that ideas exist wordlessly and can be dressed in a variety of outfits. . . . A second theory, the individualist or psychological monism, which finds its most common expression in the aphorism that the style is the man, . . . means that a writer cannot help writing the way he does, for that is the dynamic expression of his personality. . . . The most modern theory of style, Crocean aesthetic monism, is an organic view which denies the possibility of any separation between content and form . . . for the work of art (the composition) is a unified whole, with no seam between meaning and style.

The teacher who makes the first of these assumptions and who takes a dualistic view of writing or style will devote most of his freshman course to apprising his students of the various expressive means they may command, of the many ways their thoughts may be dressed. That is, he will teach composition or rhetoric as such, with relatively little concern for subject matter or what is expressed. No "particular attention [need] be paid to the substance of the writing," Milic (1965, p. 143) explains, "for the [dualistic] theory explicitly denies any link between substance and form except for logic." Teachers who subscribe to this theory of style (which he himself endorses) should be "honestly and unashamedly concerned with form and not with content," if only because their aim is to train their students to use formal devices which will serve on many different occasions to express many different contents. Courses in composition which are based on this set of assumptions or which imply this concept of style usually consist of readings in nonliterary expository prose, discussion of verbal patterns and rhetorical strategies, and a sequence of writing assignments. This is the most common course in composition: 47.5 percent of all departments begin their freshman programs with a term of straight composition and rhetoric; 23 percent devote the whole year to those subjects and to them alone. To a large extent these are the departments which see their freshman courses as service courses or as general training in verbal skills, not as preparation for further work in English. If one assumes that students can be prepared to cope with almost any writing task, one *must* assume that form can be divorced from and taught independently of content.

    Those who subscribe to one or another version of Milic's second theory (or of his third, which may be seen as an extension of the second) believe that in order to improve a student's writing one must improve his mind and give him something to say. Although they may not promise that their courses will lead to "spiritual self-improvement" (as Milic says they should if they are to meet all the demands of the "theory of psychological monism"), they are persuaded that no one can write well unless he has something to write about, and they are impressed by the fact that students' prose *does* improve when they are writing about something which interests them. Denys Thompson, former editor of the British journal *The Use of English,* expresses their conviction succinctly (1966, p. 9): "Most of us would agree that composition can be taught up to a point, that there is a need for orderly arrangement, and so on; but of late the trend has been to let training in composition take second place to ensuring that pupils have something to write about that engages them and sets their pens going. Many teachers feel that if there is an individual response to fresh and lively material, the rest will follow."

The "fresh and lively material" to which most teachers of this persuasion turn is literature. They do so not only because they are experts in literature but also because, as one chairman has written, "Imaginative literature has demonstrated, to our satisfaction at least, that it is doubly qualified as a carrier of value and a stimulus of writing." Of all the materials available to them literature is best suited, they believe, to encourage sensitivity, compassion, an awareness of irony and paradox, and other virtues which may be supposed to characterize the humanistically educated man. Furthermore, literature is portable; it comes in books which men may point to as they explore their common experiences, and the books elicit—or should elicit—complex responses which can be fully articulated only by the most careful and precise use of language. For these and other reasons 11.3 percent of all departments now devote the first term of freshman English *exclusively* to reading literature and to writing about it; 24.8 percent devote the second term to those activities; 38 percent combine literature with composition in the first term; and the same number (but not necessarily the same departments) do so in the second term.

These, then, are the polar opposites or theoretical extremes among the several types of freshman courses being offered today: the course in composition as such, which proposes to teach students to fashion conventional verbal wholes, and the course in uses of the mind, which attempts to improve writing by enlarging understanding—usually of experience as represented in literature. In theory the two are incompatible. Milic (1965, pp. 142, 143), who decries the fact that "no consistent theory of style seems to underlie the several efforts to teach composition," argues "that eclecticism will not really work and that a choice among these theories must be made by the teacher of composition." In actual practice few instructors or departments make such a choice, and many versions and combinations of the two basically antithetical courses are found. After all, papers for the course in composition must be about *something,* and papers for the course in literature must be read as compositions. Many teachers believe that it is not only impractical but wrong to make an either/or choice between the two courses, to deny themselves resources and opportunities to educate merely to achieve theoretical consistency. Anxious to give their courses substance as well as to heighten their students' sensitivity to language and form, they look for some subject matter or study that will tax the mind and contribute to an understanding of the medium and how it may be manipulated. During recent years two subjects which promise to meet these specifications have attracted some teachers of freshman English.

Linguistics

Early in the sixties it occurred to a number of teachers who had acquired some understanding of modern linguistics that the analysis of language and usage might make an ideal activity for freshman English. They themselves were intrigued by the discoveries linguists had made, and some of them thought they saw in the freshman course devoted to the study of language a way to obviate the agonizing choice between form and content. As Milic (1965, p. 144) says:

The powerful trend to the study of linguistics and substantive matters in composition courses of late years may find its source in the unconscious adoption of [the] unitary [Crocean] view. If we cannot teach rhetoric, we must teach something, but since miscellaneous social and topical subjects have produced no improvement, perhaps the final recourse to the subject matter of language itself will succeed. Thus the proponents of the linguistic readers have in a way solved the Crocean paradox. Substance cannot be separated from form, but if the substance is the form we can have the best of both worlds.

The brand of linguistics these teachers offered freshmen was, of course, very dilute. It consisted mostly of popularized essays *about* linguistics rather than actual demonstrations of linguistic analysis. Attempts were made to disabuse students of fallacious notions of "correctness" and to give them a glimpse of the complexities of modern grammars. No one who advocated these courses claimed that they would inevitably produce better prose. "My personal opinion," wrote Paul Roberts (1963, pp. 333, 335), "is that linguistic science has no cure for the problems of the composition class, so long as that class is viewed as principally a means of teaching people to write better. . . . It is not to be expected that study of the grammar, no matter how good a grammar it is or how carefully it is taught, will effect enormous improvement in writing. Probably the improvement will be small and hard to demonstrate, and for the large number of students who lack the motivation or the capacity to learn to write, it will be nonexistent." It was their business to describe, not to prescribe, the linguists continued to insist; therefore, they could hardly be expected to give practical advice to young writers.

Two difficulties immediately beset the freshman course devoted to linguistic materials: first, those materials proved much less interesting to freshmen than to their teachers; second, the number of teachers competent to speak with authority about the history and structure of the language was small. Freshmen could be titillated by such facts—now become undergraduate clichés—as the number of Eskimo words for *snow,* but more urgent concerns and appetites distracted them from the systematic study of language as such. To make that study exciting and pertinent, to devise assignments which would elicit good prose from his students, the teacher had to know more than he and his students could learn from the elementary essays in their reader. Not many did, and linguistics was therefore misrepresented and undersold. "If linguistics has not kept its promises," Francis Lee Utley (1968, p. 127) argued, "it is through no fault of its own, but because there are too few freshman teachers who are properly taught the orderly truths about their language." Those "orderly truths" are often taught to graduate students well after they have begun to teach freshmen, and they have never been taught to many teachers who left graduate school prior to, say, 1955. It is no wonder, then, that few departments have been satisfied for very long with the freshman course in linguistics and that only 4.8 percent of them now devote a whole term of their freshman program to that study.

Rhetoric

John Gerber (1967, p. 356) has derived the sudden return to rhetoric as fit matter for the freshman course from the brief vogue for courses in "communications skills" which occurred in the late forties and early fifties.

The revival of interest in rhetoric began, really, in our composition classes in the late 1940s, with the great emphasis at the time on communication skills. Designed primarily for returning veterans and largely pragmatic in purpose, most of the communication skills courses did not last long, at least at the college level, but in their short life they broke up the notion of the successful composition as a static discourse needing only unity, coherence, and emphasis for its success. Those teaching communication skills courses insisted that a written discourse must communicate something to someone. As Wendell Johnson used to say, "You don't write writing." By the late 1950s the interest in communication had broadened into a concern for rhetoric, something that our colleagues in speech had never lost. With this development came a sharper conviction that the successful composition is one that influences the thought and conduct of the reader. Accordingly, the emphasis in composition classes began to shift from logic to psychology, from form to result, from a static concept of discourse to a dynamic one. The split between the old and the new concepts came dramatically when those preparing the composition syllabus for the CEEB Summer Institutes met in Ann Arbor in the summer of 1961. Ten of those planning to direct composition courses clung to the notion of composition as logic, ten took the newer—or older—notion of composition as psychology. In subsequent conferences and in the newer textbooks, however, those espousing the dynamics of rhetoric are clearly winning out.

It was natural that English teachers should tire of the tidy but vapid compositions freshmen learn to write when all they are taught is how to play "the essay game." The great attraction of rhetoric (which has been defined by James Corbett, 1967, p. 166, as "an art governing the choice of strategies that a speaker or writer must make in order to communicate most effectively with an audience") is that it promises to be both humanistic and systematic. That is, it is concerned with humans in the act of deliberation, with choices they must make and strategies they may follow as they undertake the urgent business of communicating with their fellow human beings. But it also proposes to reduce all this to a finite body of precepts, to a system that can be taught. Thus, it seems admirably well suited to the needs of the times, being at once "dynamic" and orderly, "dramatistic" (to use Kenneth Burke's term) and pragmatic. No longer would teachers of composition simply hand their students a pattern of the coherent essay; instead, they would investigate with them the options available to men as they try to persuade others to think and see as they do. It was hoped that these options could be codified in a comprehensive rhetorical theory, which in turn would lead to more effective and more honest rhetorical practice. The years which have elapsed since the sudden vogue for rhetoric began in 1962 have not seen the fulfillment of that hope. So far there has been much talk about a "new rhetoric," and a few promising experiments in fashioning one from the insights of generative grammar and tagmemic theory have been described. But no one has yet produced the unified theory or "organon" that leaders of the movement envisioned, and the total influence on classroom teaching has probably been both superficial and slight. One obstacle confronting the partisans of rhetoric is a problem familiar to most teachers of language and its uses: how to translate theory, which describes and explains, into instruction, which offers practical advice. Robert Gorrell (1965, p. 141), who has been active in the campaign to revitalize rhetoric, candidly acknowledges this problem:

A theory of rhetoric attempts to describe accurately and consistently and fully what happens; practical rhetoric is concerned with choices. The teacher of writing is concerned with the effects of different grammatical alternatives, so that he can offer advice about which choices to make for different circumstances. In other words, rhetoric considered as practical advice about writing and speaking grows from comprehensive rhetorical theory, but it is not just a statement of theory. The problem is that when the theory gets put in practical terms, when it becomes norms or precepts, it risks being useless, being only partly applicable, and being dogmatic. . . . When the theory becomes concrete its weaknesses show.

Unless one assumes that greater understanding inevitably leads to better practice—a proposition very difficult to defend—one cannot be certain that "the new rhetoric," whenever it may appear, will necessarily result in better courses in composition and better writing by freshmen. Indeed, those who advocate a return to rhetoric seem to be headed for the same embarrassment that overtook the partisans of linguistics: the more comprehensive their theory and the more subtle and precise their analyses, the less likely they are to help the freshman who confronts the blank page. To describe *all* the rhetorical options available to him might be to render him mute; to prescribe one option over another would be to violate their theory. A major task for the new rhetoricians will be to design a pedagogy that will accommodate their theoretical deliberations to the practical exigencies of the classroom. That task they have barely begun to tackle.

Freshman Textbooks

In numbers of copies sold, freshman English is the largest single market for college textbooks: the million or more students who enroll in freshman English courses each year spend well over ten million dollars on textbooks during the first term alone. To capture this market or a sizable portion of it is the dream of many a publisher (and many an English teacher). The market is difficult to comprehend, much less to capture, however—not because freshman English is a dynamic, ever changing institution but because so many texts of a few perennial types are published and so many of them are so much alike. Teachers may choose from among some twenty handbooks of grammar, for example, and none is sufficiently distinguished to command universal adoption.

The percentage of departments using each of the standard types of texts in their freshman courses is as follows: handbooks (73.1 percent); anthologies of literature (55.6); anthologies of essays (51.5); separate literary works (48.1); rhetorics (45.1); casebooks (19.4); dictionaries (12.7); workbooks (3.7); programmed grammars (2.2); glossaries of literary terms (1.9); other, such as guides to research, speech texts, and style sheets (12.3). These figures do not vary greatly with the size, type, or geographical location of the school. They indicate that, in addition to the handbook (which many teachers now require only because they devote little or no class time to the matters it is supposed to explain), the most popular texts are still the fat anthologies, either of literary works or of "expository" prose.

It is notable, however, that almost half the departments now prefer to buy at least some of their literature in separate editions of single works rather than in large packages of preselected (and, to some extent, predigested) materials. Among departments actively experimenting with means to improve their freshman courses, the trend seems to be away from the mass adoption of omnibus anthologies and toward the varied use of individual texts selected by individual teachers. This may mean, in turn, that most teachers are devoting more effort and more imagination to devising their own courses for freshmen rather than slavishly accepting the suggestions of others. If this is true, the trend toward smaller texts may indicate a welcome trend toward diversification and experimentation in freshman English.

Innovations

Every year departments in every part of the nation ask themselves, often in tones approaching despair, "What should we do about freshman English?" If this one course or program gives them more cause for concern than any other, it is probably for three main reasons: (1) Having been acquired almost by accident, freshman English has remained an anomaly in the department's curriculum, part of it yet not part of it, demanding over a third of the department's energies yet slighted by its most eminent members, essential to the department's enterprise yet overlooked in many of its deliberations. (2) Freshman English proposes to improve students' ability to write, but no one is sure just how that can be done. (3) Unlike most other courses, freshman English has no *necessary* substance: there is no body of materials that *must* be studied to achieve its purposes, no single teaching method that *must* be practiced. Many things are possible, and often the teacher cannot predict which will be most appropriate and effective. Thus he suffers a true embarrassment of riches: because there is so much he may legitimately discuss with his students—from the nature of language to "the human condition"—he is seldom satisfied that the course he has designed is the best he might conceive and conduct.

That most departments are dissatisfied with their courses for freshmen is indicated by the fact that over 60 percent of them have recently made changes in their programs: 10.9 percent have reduced the amount of English that freshmen are required to take; 10.2 percent have reduced the amount of time devoted to grammar and the mechanics of language in their freshman courses; 8.4 percent have converted their courses in composition to courses in literature; 5.8 percent have added honors courses or special sections for students of high competence; 4.7 percent have decreed that part of their programs will be taken in the students' junior or senior years; 3.6 percent have arranged to provide more individual instruction in writing; 3.3 percent have incorporated large lecture meetings which all students attend; 3.3 percent have *increased* the amount of grammar being taught; and 29.8 percent have made other changes, ranging from instituting interdisciplinary courses to employing audiovisual aids, from discontinuing the research paper to teaching by programmed texts. Many of these innovations are minor or have been tried and abandoned elsewhere, but a few departments have introduced wholly new programs or procedures, which others may soon want to emulate or imitate. Some of the most interesting and promising major innovations to appear within recent years or decades are as follows:

Earlham's Freshman Humanities Course. Students in this course (taught by the English department alone) read a book a week and write a paper on each. The fare is varied, and teachers have no fear of venturing well outside their fields. A recent reading list included Jefferson's *Political Writings,* Joyce's *Portrait of the Artist as a Young Man,* McLuhan's *The Gutenberg Galaxy,* and Shakespeare's *Antony and Cleopatra.* Texts are chosen in the hope they will stimulate individual, original thought; no attempt is made to achieve a grand synthesis or integrated plan of studies. Writing assignments are general or "open," and the instructor tries to avoid dictating or directing class discussions. Classes (limited to about twenty students) meet three times a week to discuss the readings. In addition, students meet once a week in groups of four to six (with their instructors) to criticize each other's papers. Techniques of composition are discussed in these tutorial sessions. Obviously Earlham's program makes great demands on those who teach it, but after ten years all members of the department remain enthusiastic about the course; none regards it as a chore.

English 1 at Amherst. For over twenty years Theodore Baird of Amherst College, one of the few originals in his profession, directed a unique course for freshmen, English 1, which has had a profound influence in those who have taught it and those who have taken it. (Professor Baird retired in 1969. His course is no longer required at Amherst.) The course is difficult to describe, its "philosophy" difficult to define, in part because both are expressions of Professor Baird's singular and profoundly inquisitive mind. No textbooks are used. Classes meet three times a week, and students write a paper for *every* class. They write in response to a carefully planned series of fresh and ingenious assignments, which ask them to examine the way they act in language. As Williams Coles, Jr. (1967, p. 111), of Case Institute, who worked with Baird for several years, explains, the subject of the course "is writing, writing conceived of not as a way of saying something but as something being said, as an action, an extension of being at a moment in time." A typical initial assignment (this one by Coles) asks the students what they mean when they use the terms *professional* and *amateur*. Subsequent assignments—many of which seem merely cryptic when they are removed from the context of the course—prompt the students to recall occasions when they used the terms and to define "where they stood" and what they were doing as they used them. Papers are mimeographed and discussed in class. By posing such radical questions as "Where and how with this problem do you locate yourself? To what extent and in what ways is that self definable in language? What is this self on the basis of the language shaping it? What has it got to do with you?" the instructor hopes to develop in the student a "heightened self-consciousness of his identity as a reflex of the languages he commands."

Some teachers have complained that the course makes students so self-conscious in their use of language that they are paralyzed or reduced to inarticulateness; Professor Baird would probably reply that a good course in writing *should* make it more difficult to write. Others have said that his course teaches students only to play a special game, for which it is necessary to learn to ask a special kind of question. No one would deny, however, that the questions posed in English 1 at Amherst are of the very *best* kind: they admit of no final answers and serve only to impel a continuing activity, the activity of using the whole of one's mind as one observes oneself in the act of using language.

Freshman Rhetoric at the University of Massachusetts. Three miles away, at the other end of the town of Amherst, Walker Gibson (who once taught with Baird) recently inaugurated a new course for the thousands of freshmen who enter the University of Massachusetts each year. It combines elements of conventional rhetoric with some of Baird's emphasis on self-scrutiny. As the department's description of the course explains, "Of all student writing [it asks] three essential questions. Who are you as you make this assertion (and is this the person you want to be)? To whom are you talking (how does this awareness of audience affect your expression)? What is your evidence as you present your position or argument?" The student writes about "his own experience, especially his current university experience, his current exposure to new ways of looking." He is encouraged to experiment with a number of "voices" and to watch what happens as he shifts from one voice to another. The problem of how to teach rhetoric *and* value is met head-on:

In assessing appropriate voices proffered by our students, we will be especially suspicious of authoritarian and oversimple kinds of statements that assume a one-for-one identity between word and thing. That is, we will be attacking the familiar habit of reification—that confusion of language and reality which forgets that words are man-made and inherently abstract. The voices we hope to encourage, therefore, will be modest and self-aware, ready for change, responsive to opposing views of the question at hand.

If it works as Gibson and his staff hope it will, their course should encourage both critical awareness and honesty, twin goals of any good freshman program.

    The "Voice Project" at Stanford. Late in the summer of 1965 a group of teachers in the humanities met at Tufts University "to initiate new experiments in undergraduate instruction." Among the members of the Working Committee on English were Walter Ong, S.J., of Saint Louis University; Benjamin DeMott of Amherst; Albert Guerard of Stanford; Charles Muscatine of Berkeley; and John Hawkes, a novelist who teaches at Brown. After hearing DeMott denounce "virtually everything in literature teaching today" as "an evasion," the group set about to fashion a freshman course that would inject "a new kind of life in college teaching" and would represent a "radical innovation in education." They found the germ of such a course in a concept Father Ong (1962, pp. 52ff) had presented, somewhat cloudily, in his book *The Barbarian*

Within. "In an acceptable sense," he had written, "silent reading is a form of hearing."

Speaking and hearing are not simple operations. Each exhibits a dialectical structure which mirrors the mysterious depths of man's psyche. As he composes his thoughts in words, a speaker or writer hears these words echoing within himself and thereby follows his own thought, as though he were another person. Conversely, a hearer or reader repeats within himself the words he hears and thereby understands them, as though he himself were two individuals. . . . The speaker listens while the hearer speaks.

Evidently it occurred to those who attended the Tufts conference that they could design a course for freshmen which would encourage them to listen to their own "voices" so that they might apprehend the total personality they expressed when they used words. Whereas Walker Gibson's course at the University of Massachusetts asks students to "watch themselves" as they write, the Voice Project asked them to "listen." As it happened Albert Guerard was then in charge of freshman English at Stanford, and during the 1966–1967 academic year that university served as host to a pilot program, directed by John Hawkes and funded by the Office of Education, using "voice as a focus of multiform innovation," as Father Ong put it. One hundred of Stanford's thirteen hundred freshmen were selected to participate in the program, which also extended to the local secondary schools (Stanford students conducted "voice" experiments in elementary and high school classes) and later included a College Readiness Program for Negro students. The regular teaching staff was supplemented at times by visiting writers and experts, among them John Hersey, Jerome Bruner, and Herbert Kohl.

A good deal of what was done in class amounted to reifying Father Ong's metaphor. Students listened to recordings of their actual voices and matched what they heard with their prose on the page. They listened to other voices—Truman Capote's and that of a seven-year-old child named John Wakabayashi, for example; and they continually moved back and forth from aural to printed language, with frequent excursions into other interesting matters suggested by their explorations of the complex process of translating what is heard into what is read. Their experiment did not produce

The New Freshman Course, but it struck some good blows against that "voiceless," "mechanical" prose which most courses for freshmen, with their handbooks and their conventional assignments, seem designed to produce.

The Interdisciplinary Program at Lawrence. Lawrence University has had no freshman English since 1945. Instead, it offers its entering students an interdisciplinary (or multidisciplinary) program it calls Freshman Studies. The description of this collaborative enterprise it distributes to its freshmen begins by "defining Freshman Studies in terms of what it is not."

It is not an English class, although reading and writing are important features of it. It is not a survey of Western thought, although most of the books read in the course deal with important ideas of Western culture. It is not a "great books" course, although the books studied are great and important. Quite simply, Freshman Studies was designed to awaken students intellectually as early as possible. It also seeks to make them aware of the kind of education Lawrence tries to offer in all its departments and in its total program.

Students are required to take two trimester terms of Freshman Studies. Classes are small and meet three times a week for seventy-minute periods. Six times each term all classes meet together for a common lecture. The program is staffed by faculty members from almost all departments at Lawrence (the English department usually contributes two or three members), and "in this course all the teachers teach all the books, not merely those from their field of specialty."

The program is a kind of sampler of the principal disciplines in which the university offers instruction. It may begin one year with a three-week unit devoted to Faulkner's *Light in August,* move on to the study of a text on genetics, and then proceed to a discussion of a problem in sociology. No attempt is made to relate the several disciplines, although the faculty naturally hopes that students will perceive interconnections among the works and topics they encounter in the course. About five papers are required each term, and students are encouraged to find their own topics because their teachers "believe that students learn to write well when they have something they very much want to say." They also believe "that

the training in correct and effective writing is the responsibility of
the whole faculty and not of the English staff alone." The student
is therefore advised "not to be concerned at learning that his themes
may be graded by teachers outside the English department."

Just as they are delighted to share the burden of reading
freshman themes with their colleagues in other departments, so the
members of Lawrence's English department who approve of the
Freshman Studies program welcome the opportunities it affords to
explore disciplines other than their own. "It keeps you alive and
makes you a better teacher of English," some of them say. Others
disagree. They complain that teaching Freshman Studies makes
inordinate demands on faculty members, who must acquire at least
a superficial knowledge of subjects far outside their field of specialization. "Instead of boning up on genetics," one of them argued,
"I ought to be studying American literature, which is what I teach
best." These critics also charge that no one is fully competent to
teach the course and that requiring all faculty members who
participate to teach all the works read makes for amateurism, which
is unfair to the students. "They didn't pay their tuition to talk about
Light in August with a sociologist," one of them said. To this argument the official defense of the program replies, "The student should
understand that each of his teachers is a specialist in some one field
but is interested, as an educated man or woman, in other fields. He
will learn that liberally educated people are able to read with
intelligence and pleasure significant books on various subjects
without, of course, pretending to be specialists in them. Most especially, he should realize that his teachers, professed believers in
the liberal arts, are honestly making proof of their principles." How
well those principles are proved obviously depends on the versatility
and the dedication of the individual teacher.

Freshman Seminars

How can the department of English enrich its freshman
courses, give them intellectual substance so that they will not duplicate high school work and will confront students with urgent occasions for using language? Unknown to each other, two colleges at
opposite ends of the country—Dartmouth and Mills—have come
up with the same answer to that question. Both now require all

first-year students to enroll for one term in what are called, on both campuses, freshman seminars. These are frankly specialized courses, in which a limited topic or body of literature is studied in depth. At Dartmouth, which has a trimester calendar, freshmen take their seminar after they have had a first term of "literature and composition." At Mills freshmen may take their seminar in either of two semesters, and that is all the English they are required to take. Dartmouth allows its students a limited choice of seminars; Mills assigns its freshmen arbitrarily. Seminars at Dartmouth are limited to fifteen students, at Mills to twelve; instructors in both programs are therefore able to devote a good deal of time to individual students and their writing.

At Dartmouth members of the department who wish to participate in the seminar program (or English 2, as it is called) submit descriptions of the courses they propose to teach to the Freshman Steering Committee, which judges the feasibility of each proposal and rejects those that seem too esoteric or otherwise inappropriate. It is agreed that the same amount of writing will be assigned in all courses, but decisions on other matters—frequency and duration of meetings, classroom procedures, and the like—are left to the individual instructors. The topics and designs of most seminars derive directly from the instructors' primary professional interests or academic specialties, and a great advantage of the program is that it allows teachers—especially young teachers—to teach what they know best and find most interesting. The program also encourages experimentation and serves as a seed bed for more advanced courses. In recent years members of the Dartmouth faculty have offered seminars with such intriguing titles as The Education of the Young Man in Literature, Worlds within Worlds (a study of fantasies), and Initiation as a Theme in Fiction. One man regularly devotes the whole of his ten-week seminar to a single play by Shakespeare; students present a performance of the play at the end of the course. Freshman seminars at Mills are similarly limited in scope. One is titled The Great Romantics; another deals only with Joyce and his works. At Dartmouth (which inaugurated its program in 1958) the freshman seminars have become a well-established institution, and now other departments contribute courses that may be taken in lieu of English 2. All students are required to do the stipulated amount of writing, but their papers may now be about "Early Greek Mathematics" or "The Literature of Science" rather than "Conrad and James." In this respect Dartmouth's program resembles Cornell's Freshman Humanities Program, which will soon be described.

Albert Kitzhaber was a visiting member of the Dartmouth faculty when he conducted the investigation that resulted in his report *Themes, Theories and Therapy,* and in that book he had occasion to comment on English 2. After acknowledging that the freshman seminars had "undeniable attractions"—among them that they were "genuinely college-level courses and . . . genuinely courses in English"—Kitzhaber (1963, pp. 39–40) criticized English 2 on two counts: first, that it lacks uniformity ("When only general guides are provided for the content of such a course, there is a danger that individualism will become idiosyncrasy") and, second, that the focus of the seminars is "excessively narrow."

One may quesion whether the freshman year is the proper time for such specialization. . . . If a seminar is to deserve the name, the students in it must already have a large fund of general knowledge about the field being studied, as well as a certain amount of specialized knowledge; if they lack these qualifications, they cannot contribute usefully to the kind of discussion that is the life blood of a true seminar, nor can they profitably pursue the investigation of a special topic within the general field to which the seminar is restricted. . . . Other colleges, then, that might be tempted to introduce a course like Dartmouth's English 2, which would certainly be attractive to most English departments, should first pause to consider whether such a course does indeed serve the best interests of the freshmen who must take it— whether, that is, students are mature enough and have read widely enough by the age of eighteen to profit from a course of this sort.

Evidently neither the Dartmouth nor the Mills faculty was persuaded by these criticisms. Both testify with great conviction that their freshmen *are* competent to participate in and to profit from their specialized courses. They are aware that there can be little uniformity in their programs and that they cannot be sure that all their freshmen will learn the same things, but, as the chairman at Mills has written, "So far the advantages of the new system both in quality and morale appear greatly to outweigh any possible disadvantages." The chief advantage, they say, is that students have their first opportunity to engage in serious scholarship and to make their own discoveries, discoveries that usually pressure good, individually motivated prose. If the seminar succeeds in seizing the student's mind, he or she may learn not only much of what there is to know about a limited topic but also, as Elizabeth Pope of Mills has written, "a great deal more: that true knowledge arises not from accepting the material presented but from thinking about it; that [one] needs to think straight, to read properly, to write clearly in order for there to be any two-way traffic in ideas; that study in depth inevitably becomes study in breadth as [one] becomes aware of the interconnections of literature with anthropology, history, philosophy, psychology and sociology." When this happens, the freshman seminars, which may seem the very opposite of the general education courses popular elsewhere, may accomplish the purposes of general education as nothing else can.

Future of Freshman English

At the NCTE convention in 1959, Warner Rice of the University of Michigan read a paper with the arresting title "A Proposal for the Abolition of Freshman English, as It Is Now Commonly Taught, from the College Curriculum." It was a finely reasoned, highly cogent brief, which, if it had been widely heeded, might have dealt a death blow to an obviously infirm institution. Some of Rice's reasons for advocating the elimination of freshman English: (1) It is not—or should not be—needed. Students should acquire the competence freshman English is designed to give them before they reach college, or they should not be admitted. (2) It doesn't work. "If good habits of reading, writing, and speaking have not been inculcated before the student is of college age, it is unlikely that he will be greatly benefited by two semesters of freshman English." Students who are required to take these courses are so ill motivated, Rice said, that they seldom profit from them. (3) Eliminating freshman English would save time and money. It would also "encourage the current movement to fix responsibility for instruction in elementary subjects—language courses, mathematics up to calculus, etc.—upon the high schools; and here responsibility must increasingly reside." The lot of the college English teachers,

most of whom do not really want to teach freshman English, would
be greatly improved.

In the course of amplifying and defending his basic argument, Rice attempted to meet many of the objections he knew his
proposal would evoke: that the secondary schools are *not* doing the
job he would delegate to them (the community should insist that
they do it, he replied, and the colleges should help them); that
freshman English, though admittedly imperfect, should be improved,
not abandoned (its purposes "can be better achieved in other ways,"
he said); that freshman English is needed to support graduate students ("it ought to be possible," Rice contended, "to use many
graduate students to assist with instructional tasks more congenial
to them than composition, and for which their preparation would be
more appropriate"). He knew that it would not be easy to persuade
the rest of the faculty to consent to the abolition of freshman English "because with it must go the comfortable assumption that the
English department is solely responsible for good writing." But this
assumption is false, and it must be replaced by the truth enunciated
at Lawrence: "that the training in correct and effective writing is
the responsibility of the whole faculty and not of the English department alone." "The goal," Rice (1960, pp. 365, 366) declared,
"must be acceptance of responsibility for better English by the
whole college community. Nothing less will prove genuinely effica-
cious in the end." Having surrendered its monopoly on the teaching
of composition, the department of English should return to what it
teaches best.

*It will be asked what will replace the freshman English now taught if,
by various expedients, it proves possible to get along without it. The
answer must be a firm and emphatic: Nothing. College requirements
should simply be reduced by whatever number of hours freshman
English now absorbs. . . . There need be no question, of course, as to
the propriety of offering some English courses to first-year students.
But the English course designed for freshmen should be (as some now
are) a course in subjects which the English department is best prepared
to teach—language and literature. It should be elective, or should have
an acknowledged place in a program of general studies. Like other
courses, it should make considerable demands on the student's skill in*

reading and writing. Its purpose, like its subject matter, should be clearly defined, and clearly within the competence of those assigned to teach it.

But the inertia of departments of English is about the same as that of most institutional bodies, and so it is not surprising that Rice's eminently sensible program for reform still has not been adopted by many departments (including his own). As reported above, only about 10 percent of all departments have recently reduced the amount of English freshmen are required to take, and the number of departments which have abolished freshman English is very small indeed.

Nevertheless, there are signs that the trend among institutions of highest prestige—and eventually among those that follow their example—is toward effecting the revolution advocated by Rice. At many of these institutions members of the English department are convinced that freshmen arriving at college today are better trained in writing skills than students who entered twenty years ago. Not everyone shares this estimate, and there seems to be no way to prove it right or wrong. Although many debates over freshman English and how it can be improved founder on the precise question of just how well today's students can write and whether they need instruction in composition, it appears that no one, not even those agencies best equipped to do so, has made a historical survey of college students' verbal skills. Neither the College Board nor the Educational Testing Service has conducted such a study, but John A. Valentine, executive director of examinations for the CEEB, reports that teachers who have served as readers of the English Composition Test for many years often express the opinion that students' prose is improving, and Fred I. Godshalk, senior examiner for ETS, confirms this report. Godshalk, who believes that most students teach themselves to write, suspects that students may be more *skilled* but not better trained, that whatever improvement is noticed should probably be attributed to changes in the secondary school curriculum, which now permits students to read better works of literature at an earlier age (for example, *Moby Dick* in the tenth grade). It may well be that today's freshmen are more sophisticated than their predecessors or more adept at mimicry, but that fact alone would justify offering them a more substantial—or at least a different—freshman course.

Among the colleges and universities that have reduced the amount of freshman English students are required to take are Duke, Oberlin, and the University of Washington. Others have eliminated classroom instruction in composition. Pomona abandoned this part of its program in 1963; Chicago did so in 1966, after having required composition for twenty-five years. At Occidental College all freshmen now enroll in a general course entitled The History of Civilization, and only those whose papers for that course show serious deficiencies (or who are remanded by at least two instructors in other courses) are placed in English 1, a course in composition. In every case the principal reason given for abbreviating the freshman program or for reducing the amount of formal instruction in composition is that students' needs have changed, that most entering students no longer have an urgent need for training in composition. At these highly selective institutions, then, it would appear that Rice's vision may soon be fulfilled.

A significant number of such institutions have also converted their English courses for freshmen to courses in literature, just as he suggested. Although only 11.5 percent of *all* departments devote their freshman programs exclusively to literature, some 36 percent of the "exemplary" departments visited do so. The list includes Tulane, the University of Pennsylvania, Kenyon, the University of Buffalo, and many others. Kitzhaber noted this trend —and deplored it—in 1963. To him the return to literature seemed a self-indulgent abdication of the department's responsibility to teach composition and what he called "the principles of good writing." Those who espouse the course in literature would reply that they know of no such set of principles, that they can and do teach good writing by teaching literature, and that the multiple advantages of the course in literature more than justify substituting it for the course in composition as such. Some of those advantages Kitzhaber himself (1963, p. 97) conceded in passing; they are that "the teacher knows what he is talking about, he is likely to be enthusiastic about his subject matter, and the students have something to write about that the teacher is qualified to pass judgment on." To many English teachers at colleges and universities which

attract large numbers of the nation's best students, these seem sufficient reasons for abandoning the concept of "therapy" and for
devoting the freshman course to the finest educational experience
the department has to offer.

As it reverts to its specialty, the department must intensify
its efforts to persuade other departments to join it in teaching writing; as Rice (1960, p. 366) said, "The goal must be acceptance of
responsibility for better English by the whole college community."
Most departments of English report little progress toward that goal,
but just how it may be reached is illustrated by a major reform
inaugurated at Cornell University. In 1965 the College of Arts and
Sciences at that institution voted to abolish freshman English. For
many years it had required a term of composition and a term of
introduction to literature, but dissatisfaction with that program had
been growing, for most of the reasons reviewed above. A bold new
program, called Freshman Humanities, was instituted in 1966.
Under this plan a battery of from thirty-five to forty one-semester
courses is offered. Only about half of these are taught by the department of English; the rest are designed and conducted by other
departments in the humanities group, including history, government,
philosophy, and the fine arts. Almost all are specialized courses of
limited focus, very like the freshman seminars at Dartmouth and
Mills. Among the titles listed for the first year were American
Literature and Values, The Literature of Reason and Unreason,
and The Public Arts (taught by the department of speech and
drama). Freshmen are required to take two of these courses, one
each term of their first year. Soon after they are accepted for admission to Cornell, they are invited to select the four freshman humanities courses which interest them most, and every effort is made
to give them two of their choices. Neither need be a course in
English; if they like, they make take no English as such during their
freshman year. Thus, Cornell has effected another of Rice's reforms:
its English courses for freshmen *are* elective, and they *do* "have an
acknowledged place in a program of general studies." Mandatory
freshman English, with its captive and often dissatisfied audience,
is a thing of the past at Cornell.

The freshman course, Rice (1960, p. 366) said, "should
make considerable demands on the student's skill in reading and

writing. Its purpose, like its subject matter, should be clearly defined, and clearly within the competence of those who teach it." The beauty of Cornell's solution to the problem of freshman English is that it meets all these requirements while affording teachers in several fields opportunities to try new courses "clearly within their competence" which may engage the freshman mind. Here, as at Dartmouth, Mills, and Lawrence, a stipulated amount of writing is done in each course, and it is the duty of each teacher, whatever his field, to demonstrate by his attention to his students' papers that it *is* important to use language well to accomplish the purposes of his discipline. Meanwhile, the talents of teachers of divergent views may be enlisted, because it is not necessary for all of them to agree on some grand scheme for the education of freshmen. Among the members of any good English department there are likely to be representatives of several disparate—even antagonistic—views of writing and how it should be taught: Cornell's pluralistic program admits of a course in The Logic of Rhetoric of Expression as well as a course in Lyric Poetry. By redistributing the teaching of composition among the several departments whose disciplines put a premium on effective written expression, Cornell has probably pointed the way toward the "English" future that freshmen will take. They will take English as part of a serious study which demands the use of language. Over the nation they may write a few million fewer themes each year, but more of their themes—perhaps most—should be worth reading.

SEVEN

Interdepartmental and Special Programs

General Education

The term *general education* gained currency immediately after World War II, largely as a consequence of Harvard's well-publicized decision to institute a new multidepartmental program for undergraduates. In its 1958 report Harvard's planning committee admitted it was difficult to define the rubric it had selected:

The term general education is somewhat vague and colorless; it does not mean some airy education in knowledge in general (if there be such knowledge), nor does it mean education for all in the sense of universal education. It is used to indicate that part of a student's whole education which looks first of all to his life as a responsible human

103

*being and citizen; while the term special education indicates that part
which looks to the student's competence in some occupation.*

With no more precise definition than this to guide them the committee set about to sketch a program of nonspecialized courses, a
certain number of which all undergraduates would be required to
take. Three areas were specified: mathematics and science, the
social sciences, and the humanities. Offerings in the humanities
would include several courses in literature; as described in the
original prospectus these were to be broadly conceived introductions
to "Great Texts" and would be concerned only with "the greatest,
most universal, most essential human preoccupations." Uninhibited
by nice definitions, members of the English department refurbished
old courses and invented new ones—ranging from studies of genres
(The Epic and the Novel) through thematic courses (Problems of
Good and Evil in Western Civilization) to intensive practice in
critical reading (Reuben Brower's excellent Introduction to Literature). Eventually freshman English itself was converted to a half-
course called General Education A, a sampling of logic, rhetoric,
and literary criticism required of all Harvard and Radcliffe freshmen.

Elsewhere general education courses in the humanities
usually took the form of lofty surveys of vast expanses of cultural
history. The Humanities and Historical Studies Program, which
"comprises about a fourth of the academic work of the freshman
and sophomore years" at Grinnell College, is typical. It consists of
two one-semester courses in the humanities and two in history.
According to Grinnell's catalog,

*It provides an interdisciplinary approach to history and literature
covering the period from the ancient Greek world to the present day.
The program begins in the first semester of the freshman year, with
a humanities course on masterpieces of classical literature and history.
The courses that follow are devoted to the evolution of Western society
and to great works of our intellectual heritage, first from the Middle
Ages to the French Revolution and then in the nineteenth and
twentieth centuries. The program also includes rigorous training in
the writing of the English language. The study of masterpieces of
literature and great social documents provides the students with topics
for their papers, and the careful analysis of these prose texts fosters and*

inspires achievement in the discipline of writing. The underlying assumption is that the ability to write is associated with the ability to read.

During the first term of the humanities course, students read the Homeric epics, three Greek tragedies, some Aristotle, some Thucydides, and some Plato; during the second they study selected masterworks from Dante to Blake. Most members of the English department (as well as some members of the foreign language departments) teach this course, which serves as a substitute for freshman English. General education programs of this kind remain popular throughout the nation: about a third of all English departments participate in them. The survey of world literature is the most common general education course; next comes the humanities course, then the survey of Western civilization, then the course in the classical tradition (with much overlapping among these courses).

If the college has a general education program, all or some part of it is usually required of all students: at 37 percent of the institutions offering general education programs, all students must take all courses in the program; at 9 percent some courses are required; and at 19 percent general education courses may be used to fulfill group requirements. Most colleges and universities continue to insist that students begin their undergraduate careers with one or two years of generalized study; general education courses are designed to give those studies focus and coherence. Rather than allowing beginning students to roam among the several disciplines, gathering what understanding they may, proponents of these courses prefer to synthesize and summarize, to prepare packaged units of cultural and intellectual history for their students so that their exploratory studies will be directed and controlled. Many English teachers doubt the validity of this procedure. They are disturbed by the superficiality of general education courses, and they fear that students—many of whom are only too willing to accept "official" interpretations—will be deluded into supposing that the history of Western civilization *can* be summarized in two terms or that they "know" *The Divine Comedy* after they have spent their two weeks on Dante.

When general education replaces freshman English, the

percentage of the department's total teaching load that must be expended on lower-division courses is greatly reduced: departments participating in general education programs contribute an average of only 8.4 percent of their total efforts to those courses, whereas freshman English consumes an average of 40.7 percent. (Thus, it is not surprising that college administrators tend to favor general education programs, which seem so fortunately susceptible to mass educating by the lecture method.) But members of English departments that have acceded to the demand for general education (including the department at Grinnell) often express regret that they have consented to collaborate in an educational venture they cannot always respect.

Interdisciplinary Courses

A distinction may be made between general education programs and true interdisciplinary courses. Although the former may be interdepartmental, they need not be interdisciplinary: often the English teachers who participate teach nothing but literature, the historians nothing but history, and so on. The students are exposed to a series of experts, each discoursing on his separate specialty. In the interdisciplinary course, on the other hand, some amalgamation of two or more disciplines is attempted. Traditional boundaries between academic fields are crossed as teachers collaborate in close working teams to examine their topics more fully than the practice of a single discipline allows. Usually these efforts are prompted by the realization that the conventional distinctions among the disciplines are arbitrary and artificial and by the hope that fresh insights will be derived from bringing variously trained minds to bear on a subject. They are also designed to demonstrate to students the interrelation of the disciplines.

Of all college Engish departments, 26.7 percent participate in such interdisciplinary projects. The medium-sized college (with an enrollment of from 1500 to 2500 and an English department of from thirteen to eighteen members) seems to provide circumstances most congenial to the development of interdisciplinary courses: the faculty is large enough to supply a sufficient number of teachers willing to undertake such experiments, and the academic community is small enough to allow its members to meet. The most common interdisciplinary course is that which combines literature with history, the most literary of the other disciplines; 14 percent are of that type. Harvard has had a separate department of history and literature for many years, and that program has always attracted its share of the college's best undergraduates. Other common types are literature and religion (10.5 percent); literature, art, and music (10.5); literature and philosophy (9.3); American civilization (course, not program) (7); comparative literature (course, not program) (5.8). The remaining 43 percent of interdisciplinary courses are of assorted types, none of which is represented by more than a few examples. These include combinations of English and anthropology, English and psychology, English and sociology, English and theater, humanities and science, and journalism and sociology. Some departments reserve their interdisciplinary courses for honors students or use honors seminars as occasions for experimenting with interdisciplinary courses.

Because they usually require team teaching and small classes for their success, these courses are especially costly. That fact, the scarcity of instructors who are competent and willing to contribute to such joint enterprises, and the difficulty of effecting close collaboration among faculty members of different training and interests have inhibited the growth of interdisciplinary programs. Almost all institutions which consider undertaking curricular reforms think first of obliterating—or, at any rate, of redefining—the traditional boundaries which separate the disciplines or of redeploying the faculty to staff new courses that will more nearly address the concerns of today's students. They often find, however, that such plans are difficult to execute because academic provincialism is difficult to eradicate. The figures just presented reveal that English departments are no less parochial than others: only about a quarter of them are currently engaged in interdisciplinary projects, and those that do participate in such ventures devote an average of only 6.4 percent of their total teaching effort to interdisciplinary courses.

American Studies

The very notion of allowing undergraduates to concentrate solely on the culture of their own country seems wrong to some teachers and departments. Such specialization may be appropriate

at the graduate level, they say, but it makes no sense for undergraduates. "We see little place for an undergraduate 'major' in
American Studies, or for a B.A. degree in it," officers of the English
department at Indiana University said, "and the American Studies
Committee was in substantial agreement about this when we first
set up our graduate program." Other departments flatly disagree.
They believe that a well-planned, well-administered interdepartmental program which enables students to investigate relationships
between American literature and the history of American society
makes a perfectly legitimate undergraduate major. The department
of English at th University of North Carolina is one of these. In
1966 it inaugurated an American studies plan which illustrates the
form such programs may take. Its initial announcement described
the new curriculum as follows:

*The program is designed for students who wish to study American
life from many points of view—as it has been expressed in politics,
religion, literature, philosophy, the fine arts, urban planning, the
structure of the American economy, the press. . . . The student takes
a broad range of courses from many departments, in addition to two
special courses for majors: Introduction to American Studies, to be
taken normally in the second semester of the sophomore year, and
American Studies 80, a senior course. These courses are designed to
encourage the student to relate the information and ideas he has
acquired in his departmental courses, to notice, for example, the
relevance of the novel to politics, of urban planning to assumptions
about the good life, of philosophy and religion to the country's economic
history.*

It could be argued that programs of this kind are actually less
specialized than the conventional program for the major in English.
They permit—indeed, require—students to take "a broad range of
courses from many departments," and they encourage students to
relate what they find in literature to a variety of extraliterary matters. Not many departments have been convinced by this argument,
however, or not many institutions have felt they could afford such
programs: only 13.7 percent of all four-year colleges and universities offer American studies programs for undergraduates. The
number of students who elect the major in American studies is
very small; some departments report that no students have yet

availed themselves of opportunities for American studies advertised in their catalogs. Thus it may be said that neither English teachers nor their students have generally embraced this curricular innovation and once again their conservatism and inertia are demonstrated.

Comparative Literature

It is reliably reported (Diekhoff, 1965, p. 1) that "more people in the United States are studying modern foreign languages than ever before. They study them longer and they study more different languages. New instructional methods, new content, and new materials for the study of languages have been introduced. Teachers are more numerous and more competent." Despite these advances, which must mean that more students are coming to college today reasonably well prepared to read works of literature in languages other than English, English teachers and their colleagues in the foreign languages have almost entirely neglected another obvious opportunity for interdepartmental collaboration: only 5.6 percent of all English departments participate in true comparative literature courses for undergraduates. There are few English departments which do not teach foreign literature in translation, but very few indeed which take advantage of the undergraduate's improved competence in foreign languages to effect a fruitful comparison of works in several languages. Several large universities now offer graduate programs in comparative literature, and therefore it may be assumed that instuctors competent to teach multilingual courses are now being trained. At present, however, their competence goes almost wholly unused at the undergraduate level. The course that matches *Lazarillo de Tormes* with *Tom Jones* or the course that makes a comprehensive study of Romanticism by comparing Leopardi and Wordsworth, among others, is almost nowhere to be found.

College English teachers are not, then, a very venturesome lot. Although they tell themselves they should, they seldom leave the relatively safe grounds of their own preserve, and what innovation they contemplate or accomplish is limited, in most cases, to the confines of their own discipline or their own language. Perhaps this inclination to stay at home is a perfectly proper impulse to avoid overextending themselves as they did earlier in the century; it may also be a heritage of the New Criticism of the thirties and forties, with its salutary emphasis on attention to literature as literature. What then seemed an admirable purity may now seem mere timidity, however; and the time for excursions out of "English" into neighboring academic domains may once again be at hand. This time English teachers must be willing to give as well as take.

Teacher-Training Programs

Over three fourths of all college English departments offer or participate in teacher-training programs, so it is safe to say with Wayne Booth (1965, p. 221) that "the overwhelming majority of departments are now thoroughly committed to assuming a responsible role in the improvement of English instruction at all levels." Most of them, however, discharge this responsibility blindly, without knowing much about what it is they would improve: although 77.8 percent of all departments are involved to some extent in the preparation of teachers for the secondary schools, only 43 percent of those involved regularly communicate with schools which employ teachers of the kind they train. Those departments that have effected such "articulation" with the schools have used the following means: 23.9 percent hold or attend conferences and workshops; 15.7 percent (of English departments, not of departments or schools of education) supervise practice teaching; 2.2 percent make occasional, informal visits to the schools; and 17.9 percent rely on other means, such as advanced-placement programs, literary contests, film programs, and "college nights." Departments in large public universities are more likely to have established such communication—55 percent of them have done so—but a higher-than-average number of these (about 85 percent) offer teacher-training programs. The general picture is of a profession whose right hand does not know what its left hand is doing, a situation that James Squire (1968, p. 527) has rightly deplored:

I can no more conceive of a truly effective preparatory program being controlled by a faculty without direct contact with schoolteachers than I can conceive of an effective school English program without direct contact with scholars of English. Our subject is no simple body of content and theory to be walled away from today's social, cultural, and educational concerns. . . . No development will sooner undercut much that we have achieved in American education than a retreat of college departments from assuming their share of responsibility for the entire spectrum of English instruction.

Most department chairmen would agree with this assertion; most are apologetic for neglecting the very schools they serve. In self-defense, however, they would remind their critics that it is extremely difficult to find college teachers of English who are genuinely interested in the problems of the secondary schools and who are willing to devote part of their professional careers to helping the schools. With Jeremiah S. Finch (1965, p. 4) they would point to "a state of mind which prevails widely in departments of English."

In extreme form it is found in those who profess total indifference toward education below the collegiate level. The more common manifestation of this state of mind is found among our less austere colleagues who protest that they are concerned about the public schools but do little or nothing to demonstrate it. Their views are likely to be a curious blend of distrust and apathy, all too often based—in most unscholarly fashion—on inadequate or inaccurate evidence. The irony is that many of these very people are themselves dwelling in houses which are not in good order.

The majority of departments must assume that their training programs will somehow contribute to the improvement of teaching, whether or not they are nourished by direct contact with the schools. At any rate, they continue to offer such programs, in response to heavy demand: the major in the teaching of English remains among the three most popular majors at 76 percent of all colleges and universities; indeed, it is slightly more popular across the nation than the regular major in English.

The English department's contribution to the major in teaching varies greatly among four-year colleges and universities; some departments (18.9 percent) conduct their own programs, supplying instruction not only in language and literature but also in teaching methods; others (77.8 percent) cooperate with departments or schools of education to produce teachers who will meet local certification requirements. In other words, less than a fifth of

those English departments which contribute to the preparation of
teachers conduct their own programs; the rest collaborate with
departments or schools of education in joint programs. Closer
examination of programs administered solely by English departments
helps to explain why such collaboration is often difficult to maintain.

In the matter of who is permitted to major in teaching
there is no great disagreement: almost any student in good standing
may qualify, either for the English department's program or for
the education department's. When the English department designs
and controls its own program, it usually imposes no requirements
for admission: 63.3 percent of those that have their own programs
admit all who wish to enter. Others (40.3 percent) require freshman English, but this is not a special requirement because on most
campuses all students must pass that course. In 30.7 percent junior
status is required, in 29 percent sophomore status. Knowledge of a
foreign language is required by 24.2 percent, special matriculation
by 4.8 percent. When a specific grade-point average is required, it
is usually a C. But the achievement of junior status and a C average,
the most common combination of requirements, does not distinguish
the teaching major from most other majors. English departments,
then, do not apply special criteria when they select candidates for
the teaching degree; certainly those who study for that degree under
their auspices are not members of an elite.

Once they have been admitted to a teacher-training program administered by the English department, students take an
average of thirty credit hours of required courses. This figure (which
may not be perfectly valid because of the difficulty of defining a
"credit" and of comparing programs at institutions which have
different academic calendars) is lower than the average number
of credit hours required when the teacher-training program is
conducted by the school of education (33.5) and lower than the
average number required for the regular major in English (37.6).
It would seem, then, that English departments demand less of their
majors in teaching than they do of their regular majors but also
less than schools of education demand of *their* majors who are
preparing to teach English.

Some sense of what departments of English consider an
appropriate set of courses for the major in teaching may be derived

from the following statistics: a course in Shakespeare is required by 70.2 percent of departments, a survey of American literature by 68.1 percent, a course in linguistics by 59.6, advanced composition by 55.3, a survey of English literature by 48.6, period courses by 38.3, a course in teaching methods by 34, a course in literary criticism by 19.2. Courses of several other types, such as Middle English, modern literature, and speech, are sometimes also required; but none of these courses is required by over 15 percent of all departments. When this list is compared with a list of courses most commonly required for the regular major in English, the following differences appear: requirements for the regular major include more courses in literature and literary criticism (for example, the survey of English literature is required for the regular major by 74.8 percent of all departments, for the major in teaching by only 48.6 percent); on the other hand, Shakespeare is more frequently required in teacher-training programs than in regular programs. Linguistics and advanced composition are required in about 60 percent of training programs to about 35 percent of regular programs. In general, then, this comparison confirms one's impression that prospective teachers are asked to take more "practical" courses and fewer "liberal" courses than regular majors in English.

Is the typical program one may infer from this list of requirements an *appropriate* course of studies for students who are preparing to teach in the schools? Will it give them the knowledge and skills they need to become competent teachers? Since 1967, when the English Teacher Preparation Study (sponsored by the National Association of State Directors of Teacher Education and Certification, NCTE, and MLA) published its "Guidelines for the Preparation of Teachers of English," it has been possible to identify most of the competencies teachers of English should have and to approach an evaluation of existing or proposed teacher-training programs. Although the authors of this report were careful to state (p. 21) that it was not their intention to "identify in any detail . . . specific courses which might exist within a program or the arrangement of such courses, [or to] attempt to prescribe the specific number of credit hours in English required for adequate preparation," it is legitimate to compare the generalized recommendations of the study with the analysis of English departments' requirements for the degree in teaching. Such a comparison reveals that many English departments which offer their own teacher-preparation programs do not now follow the study's guidelines and do not meet many of the standards it recommends. Thus, the report states (p. 24) that "the teacher of English at any level should have . . . an understanding of the nature of language"; that is, as its amplifying remarks make clear (p. 24) "he should have some understanding of phonology, morphology, and syntax . . . [and] should be well grounded in one grammatical system and have a working acquaintance with at least one other system." In order to acquire familiarity with these matters, most students will need a college course in linguistics, but, as we have seen, only 59.6 percent of all English departments which conduct their own teacher-training programs now require such a course. Similarly, the guidelines prescribe (p. 24) "instruction in writing beyond the college freshman level, either through an advanced course in composition or through supervised individual instruction and practice." But advanced composition is now required in only 55.3 percent of teacher-training programs administered by departments of English. The most obvious discrepancy between English department practice and the study's recommendations concerns the course in teaching methods. The report flatly states that "the teacher of English at any level should have studied methods of teaching English," but when English departments are left to design their own programs for the major in teaching, only 34 percent of them require the methods course. Obviously the English departments' faith in the value of teaching teaching is not much greater than it ever was, despite the educationists' continued insistence on the need for such training.

My survey did not examine programs for training teachers of English conducted solely by departments or schools of education. I did determine, however, that although such programs are heavily influenced by the certification requirements of the several states and although they almost invariably devote some time to courses in methods, they may require *more* subject-matter courses in English than programs conducted by the English departments themselves. In addition to courses in education and related fields (for example, child psychology), students in school of education programs are required to take an average of 35.5 credit hours in English, slightly more than is usually required by the department of English of its majors in teaching, slightly less than is required of its regular majors. For college teachers of English these are humbling facts. They indicate that the schools of education, to whom the English faculty has sometimes been reluctant to entrust the training of the teachers who will prepare its undergraduates, may now be doing a better job at that task than they themselves can or will do when it is left to them.

EIGHT

General Curriculum

Courses for Nonmajors

Well over half the students enrolled
in sophomore, junior, and senior courses in English are *not* majors
in English: the average percentage of nonmajors in courses above
the freshman level is 55.8. Students specializing in English account
for a majority of enrollments in courses above the freshman level at
only 37.9 percent of all institutions; at all the rest they are a
minority. The proportion of majors to nonmajors in courses above
the freshman level varies somewhat with the size and type of school:
the smaller the school, the more probable it is that the majority
will be nonmajors, which may mean that English is more popular
among nonmajors at small schools than large. For some reason,
nonspecialists are in the majority at more private than public or

sectarian schools, even though private schools are *least* likely to require English courses above the freshman level. There are two principal reasons for the preponderance of nonmajors in these courses: the first is that most institutions—63.7 percent, to be exact —do not ask their students to declare their majors until the end of the sophomore year or later, and therefore there are no majors in sophomore courses—*all* students in courses at that level are considered to be nonmajors; the second is that 81.7 percent of all colleges and universities require or encourage all students to take a year of English beyond the freshman level. At 43.1 percent of all institutions a second year of English is mandatory; at 38.6 percent English courses may be used to fill "group" or "distribution" requirements. The result is that the department's sophomore courses, like its freshman classes, are populated very largely by representatives of what Harold Martin has called "the commonwealth of students," and its obligation to those students is very great.

Twenty-three percent of all departments meet this obligation by distinguishing between courses for majors and those for nonmajors; normally the latter may not be used to fulfill the requirements for the major. Thus, the English department at Pomona College offers a sophomore course entitled Great Authors, which is specially designed "for students who do not intend to concentrate in English"; it offers another course, Major English Poets, for those who do. At the University of Kentucky a sophomore course in American literature may not be counted toward the major; it is reserved for nonmajors. These courses usually require less specialized reading and fewer papers on easier topics than courses for the major. At the University of Washington, for example, sophomore courses for nonmajors survey types of literature and selected works of great writers, while courses for majors examine literary history in greater detail. Classes in the latter are smaller, and grading standards are higher. Departments which differentiate in this way believe they must do so if they are to meet the different educational needs of specialists and nonspecialists. Others oppose such segregation, fearing that it may encourage premature specialization and may result in homogenized classes which prevent fruitful communication among students of different interests and abilities. It is not a bad idea, they think, to mix the engineers in with the English majors, at least in lower-division classes. Much depends, of course, on how competent and how articulate the engineers may be.

Over a third of all departments (36.6 percent) offer specially planned sequences of courses for students whose minor is English. In most cases these are regular courses, open to all students, which are considered by the English department to be especially appropriate supplements to the intensive study of other disciplines. The survey of English literature, for example, is often recommended to majors in history. Shakespeare and advanced composition may be suggested for majors in the sciences (if they are permitted to take *any* courses outside their fields of concentration). In this way departments hope to improve the counseling of nonmajors and also, perhaps, to control the enrollments in their general courses.

The courses most often recommended for nonmajors are the survey of English literature (by 38.2 percent of all departments), world literature (by 26.7 percent), and the survey of American literature (by 23.7 percent). From the fact that no more than two fifths of all departments recommend any one course it is clear that there is no consensus as to which course constitutes a proper sequel to freshman English. Apparently there is agreement only on the nature, not on the substance, of the courses nonmajors should be urged to take: almost all the courses recommended are broad surveys, which proceed at a rapid pace through centuries of literary history, with time allowed for the reading and discussion of only a few exemplary works. Before it releases him for specialization elsewhere, then, the English department attempts to discharge its responsibility to the nonmajor by giving him a panoramic or synoptic view of its wares and perhaps a summary account of what happened in the history of one body of literature. It does so on the assumption that such generalized courses will do him most good, that they will at least provide him with some "background" (even though he may never have the time or the inclination to examine the foreground of the subject) and that education for nonspecialists should probably consist of wide coverage rather than intensive study.

That this assumption should now be reconsidered is suggested by a comparison of the list of courses which are recommended for nonmajors with a list of those courses which are most frequently *elected* by them. Following are the courses that regularly attract large numbers of nonmajors when they are free to choose their own (figures are the percentage of departments citing each course; many cite more than one): survey of American literature (51.8); Shakespeare (46.9); modern literature (22.8); modern novel (21.4); modern drama (20); survey of English literature (18.8); world literature (14.9). Only one course which is commonly prescribed ranks high on this list of courses which are most popular with nonmajors: the survey of American literature. The next four entries—Shakespeare and the several varieties of modern literature —are seldom recommended when a second year of English is required. In other words, there is a manifest discrepancy between the type of studies in English nonmajors most commonly choose for themselves and the type which is most frequently selected for them. When the choice is left to them they tend to elect courses which appear to have immediate pertinence to their own lives (courses in American or modern literature) or courses of relatively narrow focus (Shakespeare or the genre courses), not the wide-ranging surveys of the literature of the past their elders think right for them.

Curriculum above the Freshman Level

About 80 percent of the courses that departments of English offer to sophomores, juniors, and seniors can be classified under ten general headings. The categories overlap to some extent, and the process of classification inevitably obliterates some distinctions and misrepresents some courses. For the purposes of comparing large numbers of curriculums and of defining recurring patterns, however, the following designations will serve: *courses in works of individual authors* (Chaucer, Shakespeare, Milton, as well as courses in the works of two or three authors—for example, Conrad and James); *American literature* (survey and period courses in literature by American authors); *genre courses* (poetry, drama, the short story, and the novel, taught as such); *period courses* (specific periods or episodes in the history of literature—for example, the eighteenth century or the Victorian period); *linguistics* (advanced grammar and the history of the English language); *survey courses* (chronological reviews of the history of English literature); *masterworks courses* (chronological reviews of limited numbers of masterpieces or master authors); *advanced composition* (expository writing, sometimes with attention to theories of composition and rhetoric); *creative writing* (practice in imaginative writing); *literary criticism* (studies in critical theory).

Almost all departments offer some courses that do not fit into these categories—courses in folklore, for example, or in teaching methods—but most of their offerings above the freshman level are of these types. Classifying them in this manner makes it possible to determine how many departments teach how many courses of each common type. The following list indicates the percentage of departments offering courses of each kind: individual authors (95.6 percent; two one-term courses most common); American literature (94.1; two courses); genres (93.4; four courses); periods (91.6; four courses); linguistics (79.5; one course); survey of English literature (78.4; two terms); advanced composition (72.2; one course); creative writing (71.1; one course); literary criticism (67; one course); masterworks (26.1; two terms). These figures help to explain the apparent uniformity of college curriculums in English: they reveal that at least two thirds of all departments offer at least one course in each of the categories we have defined (except the course in masterworks, which is often seen as an alternative to the survey course). Departments may disagree on how *many* courses of each type they should offer, but most of them try to ensure that all the standard types will be represented in their curriculums. Thus, their catalog listings look much alike. Almost all contain a course in Shakespeare, some American literature, three or four genre courses, and several courses in the literature of separate periods (and almost all define those periods alike).

But although there is much sameness in curriculums above the freshman level, they have not remained wholly unchanged during recent years. In particular, many of them have been expanded or modified to include more units of such nonliterary subjects as linguistics, the history of the language, and advanced composition. An NCTE survey conducted by Harold B. Allen in 1960 found that only 28 percent of departments in four-year colleges and universities offered courses in modern English grammar, and only 58 percent had courses in the history of the language; in 1968 almost 80 percent had courses in one or both of these subjects. Another survey conducted in 1960 reported that one third of these departments did *not* offer advanced composition; that figure has dropped to 27.8 percent. The quality of many of these offerings may be questioned, because the number of teachers who are competent to conduct substantial courses in linguistics and rhetorical theory remains limited. Evidently most departments have decided, however, that a comprehensive curriculum should include courses of these types, whether or not they are heavily subscribed and properly taught.

The department's ability to supply courses of the several types depends largely on its size and the demand for English on its campus. My statistics on how many courses of each type are usually offered by departments of each size yield some valuable insights, one of which is that the number and variety of courses offered do not increase in direct proportion to the size of the department. Large departments may slice their subject matter into somewhat smaller portions—may offer more period, genre, and "other" courses, that is—but they do not offer many more courses of most of the standard types. A department which has eight members and which serves a student body of one thousand may be expected to provide three courses in the works of individual authors, and so may a department which has twenty-eight members and serves a student body of five thousand. The large department may offer more sections of popular courses (depending on how large it allows its classes to become), but its battery of courses will not be much more diversified than that of the small department.

There is a limit to the number of survey (or masterworks) courses that need be offered, because such courses are designed to summarize the whole of English or American literature in a few terms. Most departments find that two one-term courses of this type are sufficient (although those offering surveys of both English and American literature may have from four to six courses in all). Courses of other types are limited by the demand or by the available competence of the staff. Few departments offer more than three terms of advanced composition, of creative writing, or of literary criticism. Evidently it is felt that an adequate curriculum for undergraduates need include no more than a few one-term courses of each of these types.

From the data I collected, it was also possible to derive a more or less accurate blueprint of the curriculum in English above the freshman level in the typical department. It will be remembered that just about half of all English departments have fewer than ten members. Departments of this very common size are often found to present the following array of one-term courses for sophomores, juniors, and seniors: two or three courses in the works of individual authors (usually Chaucer, Shakespeare, and Milton); two courses in American literature (usually two terms of a survey course extending from colonial to modern literature); four courses in literary genres; four or five courses in the literature of separate periods (typically the Renaissance, the eighteenth century, the Victorian period, and the modern period); one or two courses in linguistics or the history of the language; two terms of a survey or masterworks course; one course in advanced composition; one or two courses in creative writing (often a course in writing short stories and a course in writing poetry); one course in literary criticism; three courses of other types (for example, world literature, the Bible as literature, or speech).

The curriculum in English offered in 1967–68 at Lawrence University (which had 1290 undergraduates, an English department of eight members, and a trimester calendar) illustrates this pattern almost exactly. It consisted of the following courses (listed as they appeared in the catalog):

Introduction to English Literature (masterworks; two terms)
Expository Writing (advanced composition)
Literary Forms and Types (practical criticism)
Public Speaking
Literary Composition (creative writing; two courses)
American Literature (survey; two terms)
Introduction to Shakespeare (nonmajors)
Studies in Shakespeare (majors; two terms)
Milton and the Seventeenth Century
Chaucer and His World
Eighteenth-Century Literature
The Romantic Movement
The Victorian Age

The English Novel
Renaissance Literature
Modern Fiction
Modern Poetry
The English Language
Literary Criticism
Introduction to Linguistics
Tutorial Study for Seniors (one or more terms)
Independent Study in English (honors projects)

This program represents a kind of epitome or paradigm of curriculums now offered across the nation. Very large departments may offer more courses (in 1968 the largest, at Illinois, had eighty-three to Lawrence's twenty-six), but most of these are refinements on basic types (for example, Illinois offers three separate courses in the English novel—English Novelists of the Eighteenth Century, English Novelists of the Ninteenth Century, and The Mid-Victorian Novel —to Lawrence's one). English departments, then, may enlarge their lists of courses as they themselves grow larger and serve more students, but they seldom add courses of wholly new types.

Teaching Procedures

Lawrence's entirely typical program serves to "cover" most of the subjects and bodies of literature English teachers have traditionally considered the prime matter of their discipline. It does not do much more than that. What renovation and innovation are accomplished must therefore be effected by individual teachers working within the confines of their conventional curriculum. Fortunately, teaching conditions at Lawrence—and at many other colleges and universities—still permit that fertile exchange of ideas and perceptions which may refresh even the most stereotyped course. When I investigated the teaching procedures employed in courses of all kinds at institutions of all types, I found that, like Lawrence, the great majority of departments provide opportunities for discussion in most of their classes. The straight lecture is the least common teaching procedure: even such technical subjects as linguistics are taught by this method in less than one fifth of all departments. Discussion groups are more common than lectures, but the most common method is some combination of both. It is impossible to tell just how much time is allotted to each; perhaps many of these courses include little more than a question period at the end of each class as a gesture toward discussion. The large lecture followed by sectioning into smaller discussion groups is not very common, unless that procedure is masked in the large percentage of courses said to be taught by a combination of lecture and discussion.

Not surprisingly, lecturing is more common in large institutions than in small, but the degree of difference is less than one might expect, and the incidence of lecture/discussion classes does *not* vary in direct proportion to size. Medium-sized private colleges seem to afford most opportunities for discussion in courses of all types—perhaps because such institutions are still committed to a tradition of individual instruction and have large enough faculties to maintain that tradition.

Class Size

That teachers resort more and more to lecturing, without discussion, as classes grow larger is confirmed by my findings. But the average percentage of departments conducting courses of *any* type by the lecture method alone never exceeds 19; no matter what the course, less than 20 percent of all departments teach it by lecturing. This heartening fact may be related to another, which some will find truly surprising: the most common undergraduate class above the freshman level contains from ten to twenty-nine students. Large classes in English are quite uncommon: only 5.1 percent of all departments have *any* classes of over seventy-five students, and only 3.1 percent have any of over one hundred. When I related class size to several variables—type, size, and location of school—I discovered that the class of fewer than twenty students is the most common at most institutions. Indeed, at 38 percent of all institutions the typical class *above* the freshman level is no larger than the average section of freshman English. Large departments at large institutions do allow their classes for sophomores, juniors, and seniors to grow beyond the size of their classes for freshmen, but very few of them report that classes of from forty to forty-nine students are most common on their campuses, and *none* reports that classes of over fifty are typical. Enrollment modes are slightly higher at public than at private and sectarian institutions, but again they are much lower than might be expected: 61.8 percent of all public schools report that their typical classes contain fewer than thirty students.

There is nothing sacrosanct about the small class, of course. It is costly, and, if the teacher's purpose is simply to impart information or explanation, it may be wasteful. The office of the English teacher, however, is not only to inform and to explain but also to initiate and to sustain an interchange of thought, feeling, and judgment. This he cannot do well in classes of over, say, forty students. Larger classes inhibit students or make it impossible to entertain their responses at length. Administrators who argue that a few more students per class can't hurt should be reminded that it is difficult to discuss more than a sonnet an hour with a fully responsive class of twenty. Not all students welcome such small classes; many would prefer to sit at the feet of a lecturer, happily filling their notebooks with official interpretations and evaluations. All but the most vain teachers of English know, however, that to indulge such students is to leave their job half done. Not to worry their students into responses and to orchestrate their responses into something better than any one member of the group brought into the classroom would be like clapping with one hand. But if contact is to be made, both hands must be in proximity, and this can be accomplished only in small classes. Fortunately, these are still common on American campuses.

Papers and Examinations

Most undergraduate courses in English afford opportunities for written as well as oral expression: at least one paper per term is required in about 95 percent of all courses, no matter what the type. The number of essays or writings assigned may reach as high as ten in courses in advanced composition or in creative writing, but the most common practice is to require a single term paper. Many teachers would now argue that this is bad practice. The writing assignments for an undergraduate course in English, they believe, should be conceived not as tests of the student's erudition or final "command of the subject" but as occasions for articulating his developing perceptions. They would prefer to assign a number of shorter papers throughout the term rather than a single climactic essay. This tendency toward refracting the writing required into small units distributed throughout the term seems consistent with that view of undergraduate study in English which sees it as a continuous activity rather than as a march toward some well-defined goal. Teachers of this persuasion think it less important that students make a "final" statement before leaving the course than that they remain verbally active while they are acquiring their understanding of the subject.

Some test of what the student has acquired is still considered necessary by most teachers, however, if only because they must submit grades at regular intervals. The hour examination at mid-term and the two-hour final remains the most common program of tests, the essay question the most common testing device. Happily, there does not seem to be any significant trend toward greater use of machine-graded examinations, despite their popularity elsewhere. Most English teachers are well aware that the essay test itself is a highly fallible instrument, and they have no desire to substitute even more dubious devices.

The undergraduates' essays and examination papers are usually read and evaluated by the teachers who assigned them. Of all departments, 45.7 percent employ assistants to help in correcting papers and examinations, but their office is usually limited to checking students' prose for mechanical errors. Two thirds of the departments that rely on such assistance employ undergraduates—usually seniors majoring in English; the rest use graduate students or other members of the community. Some departments assign assistants on the basis of enrollments: one "reader" may be provided for every thirty students over the normal enrollment. But fortunately such overpopulated classes are rare, and the practice of farming out the students' written work—a practice very few teachers or students find satisfactory—is not widespread.

This description of the conditions under which English is taught to American undergraduates and of the procedures endorsed by most departments suggests that if the subject is taught badly, it is probably the fault of individual instructors and their methods, not of institutions which oppress them. Most teachers continue to enjoy the luxury of small classes, most are encouraged by the policies and traditions of their departments to engage their students in discussion and to have them write. Some may charge that they are asked to teach too many classes and to read too many papers; others, that conventional curriculums stifle innovation. But except for these complaints—which should not, of course, be dismissed—there seem to be few occasions for blaming the state of instruction in English on external circumstances. The embarrassing truth is that most teachers of English probably get from their students just about what they deserve.

NINE

The Major in English

Somewhere between 6 and 10 percent of all undergraduates in the United States are majors in English; the average percentage among institutions of all sizes and kinds is 7.8. More precise figures disclose that the major in English is most popular at small colleges, at sectarian and private schools, at noncoeducational institutions (many of which are colleges for women), and at schools in the North Atlantic section of the nation. The same pattern is revealed when the percentages are computed in another way: a higher-than-average proportion of the total student body majors in English at about 40 percent of small schools as compared to about 18 percent of large; at about 40 percent of sectarian as compared to about 22 percent of public; at about 30 percent of noncoeducational as compared to about 22 percent of coeducational schools; and at about 40 percent of the schools in the North Atlantic states as compared to about 5 percent in the southeastern states.

The small percentage of the total undergraduate body which

majors in English may be misleading. Among the many different majors now being offered, English is still one of the three most popular on three quarters of the nation's campuses. At one third of all institutions it is the *most* popular major, at another 20 percent it is the second most popular, and at 22 percent the third. Its chief rival varies from campus to campus and from year to year: it may be history, or the life sciences, or some other discipline, depending on local traditions, the popularity of individual faculty members, the social concerns of the moment, and other factors. Even at large schools which offer many choices, however, English remained enormously popular for many years: in 1967 it ranked first at 40 percent of institutions of this size. How long it will retain that position is now a question. In 1972 Michael F. Shugrue reported that one major private university, with eight thousand students in the liberal-arts college, suffered a 20 percent decline in English majors in one year, and I have heard similar reports from many other institutions. Evidently the trend away from English and humanities toward more practical disciplines has already begun to affect the major.

The great majority of students who elect to concentrate in English are women. The average percentage of males among English majors at coeducational institutions is 31.5; that is, female majors in English outnumber males by over two to one. Even at such institutions as the University of Chicago, where the student body as a whole is predominantly male, over two thirds of the majors in English are women. It is worth noting, however, that the opposite is true at most Canadian coeducational institutions. There the major in English usually attracts more men than women. This difference may be due in part to the fact that there is still no tradition of higher education for all qualified women in that country and therefore Canadian colleges and universities enroll many more men than women. But it also suggests that Canadian students may not subscribe so readily to the notion prevalent among Americans that English is an effeminate discipline, fit only for women who intend to teach the very young. That view (which may be more common in the Midwest and South than in other parts of the United States) continues to plague some English departments, which complain that their upper-division classes are populated largely by docile young ladies who make dutiful but somewhat dull pupils. Members of these departments wish they could persuade more young men that their programs for the major in English may be just as challenging to the male intellect as the major in chemistry or economics.

Although they may lament the imbalanced distribution of the sexes among their majors, very few English departments now have cause to deplore their general quality. The majority (64.6 percent) of departments report that their programs for the major attract a representative group, including students of every competence; 31.9 percent say their majors, with a few exceptions, are the most competent students at their institutions; and 2.7 percent say they enlist *only* the very best students. No department rates its majors uniformly mediocre or inferior, and only 9.5 percent report that they are forced to lower standards to accommodate incompetents. Apparently the day is past when English served as a refuge for dilettantes, "gentleman C" students, and those who had failed at other disciplines. Most teachers would agree with the chairman at Pomona, who said in an interview, "The college is getting better and better students, and we get our share of the best." On many campuses English is known as a "tough major": the department's standards are high and its requirements more rigorous than those of other departments. This serves to discourage most of the non-committed students who might otherwise seek in English an easy route to the degree. Not all of those who do enroll in its program for the major are fully committed when they begin, but most can muster a genuine interest in literature and are therefore worthy of the special attention they receive.

At 55.3 percent of all institutions students choose their major late in the second half of their sophomore year. The faculties of these colleges usually subscribe to the traditional belief that the student's first two years should be devoted to exploring a variety of disciplines and to developing new interests. This belief has recently been challenged at a number of institutions; now 22.9 percent ask students to declare their majors at the end of the freshman year, and 16.8 percent require them to do so upon entering. Typical of the latter is the Washington Square College of New York University. There the faculty voted in 1964 to abandon an elaborate set of distribution requirements which obliged all students to take courses in almost every discipline before they were allowed to major. Now students declare their majors as soon as they arrive at the college. If they choose English, they become, in effect, apprentice majors or candidates for the major and are placed in special sections of freshman English (called colloquia and limited to twenty students per class). They must take two terms of this course; if they receive Ds in both, they are not allowed to continue in the program for the major.

Members of the English department believe their new plan works well with the highly competent students the Washington Square College admits. Formerly, they say, their lower division students spent their first two years acquiring a smattering of many subjects; now they may proceed directly to the intensive study of those subjects which interest them most, and the freshman colloquia in English serve as "a way to find out early whether the student's interest can stand some strain." To English teachers at several other institutions (for example, at Swarthmore, which is as highly selective as NYU), it seems wholly mistaken to encourage, much less to demand, such early majoring. They fear overspecialization and parochialism as programs for the undergraduate major in English come to look more and more like programs of graduate studies. A compromise policy which many schools now endorse permits a few unusually well-qualified students of demonstrated dedication and ability to declare their majors early. Of all departments, 48.6 percent now allow such students (who are usually identified by their own requests and by outstanding work in their first term) to choose their majors in their freshman year, and most of them assign these precocious majors to counselors in the English department, who offer them special advice to ensure that the courses they take as sophomores will prepare them properly for concentration in English.

Admission Requirements

About 42 percent of departments impose no restrictions on admission to the major in English, accept all students who wish to enroll in their programs; 13.7 percent reserve the right to refuse admission at the discretion of the department and depend on their own ability to dissuade weak students; another 12.8 percent rely on the reputation of the major to eliminate such students. The most common formal requirement is a certain grade-point average, either in English or in all courses: 11.6 percent of the institutions with formal requirements require a C average, 22.4 percent a C+. One department in Texas has deliberately lowered its barrier to C− because, as the chairman said, "We know that if they don't major with us they will major in education, and we think we can make better school teachers than the educationists can, no matter how bad the student."

If most English departments are inclined to entertain all students who profess a serious interest in their subject, it is probably not because they hope to save them from education or any other major but because members of these departments are aware that, as trustees of a discipline central to all humane studies, they have no right to exclude any who would partake of it. It is difficult to identify any special aptitude which is essential to success at the practice of this discipline, and most English teachers have no desire to limit admission to their major to students of any one type. They prefer to welcome a heterogeneous group and then to offer them a properly demanding—and rewarding—course of studies.

Programs for the Major

When they turned to describing programs for the major in English—specifically, which courses in literature were required by how many departments and at what levels—an earlier team of surveyors, Donald R. Tuttle and Helen O'Leary (1965, p. 40), confessed their bewilderment: "The number of course titles seems myriad; the ways of organizing materials are numerous indeed; and the changes and counterchanges are so numerous and seemingly so contradictory that it is hard to organize the body of data in a way that will display whatever meaning it contains."

The components of such programs are not difficult to identify: as I have said, most English courses above the freshman level can be classified as examples of ten basic types. These are the blocks of which the major is made, but it is amazing how many different structures can be designed. One department will build its major on a foundation of survey courses; another will construct its program entirely of smaller units. One will insist on so many units of early literature; another will permit almost any combination of courses. Where to put the course in Shakespeare is a small but important question which divides departments: some require it in the sophomore year; others postpone it until the senior year. Often departments at very similar institutions are found to have very different programs, for reasons difficult to discern. Examples are Wesleyan and Dartmouth. Both are wealthy, highly selective New England colleges. They draw their students from the same secondary schools, and, what is more important for this comparison, they recruit their faculty from the same graduate schools. Yet Wesleyan puts great emphasis on its survey courses, which are required of all majors, and Dartmouth will have none of such courses. Each is convinced that its practices are correct and considers its plan for the major wholly appropriate. The many arguments for and against the survey course—all of which have been rehearsed on many occasions in meetings of each department—lead to fundamental questions about the study of literary history (see below), but such questions these nearly identical departments answer differently.

The great variety or confusion of programs for the major in English points to one of two conclusions: either departments of English have not faced up to the task of deciding just what constitutes an essential plan of studies for undergraduates who would specialize in their discipline, or that decision cannot be made and that plan cannot be devised because their discipline cannot be defined. There have always been those who have thought that English teachers should be able to agree on what constitutes a proper set of courses for the major and therefore that some common program should be endorsed by most departments. In 1954 Thomas Clark Pollock (p. 330) wrote: "The major should give the student the opportunity to concentrate on a carefully organized program of studies in the particular department he has chosen for his specialization. The emphasis should be on careful, thoughtful organization of the major program as distinct from a major program which is

not carefully planned or is disorganized or haphazard. The major
should *lead* somewhere." And more recently Wayne Booth has proposed a general reform of undergraduate programs which would
correct the drift toward the "nonprograms" he finds prevalent.
Booth's argument, presented in the chapter he contributed in 1965
to *The College Teaching of English,* assumes that consensus may be
reached on which "skills departmental programs ought to develop"
(p. 203), that "all worthwhile educational planning includes provision of sequences" (p. 214), and that it should be possible therefore
"to design programs that will lead every student, regardless of his
special field, to develop these skills" (p. 202). He concedes that
"English is an especially amorphous subject, requiring repeated
efforts at definition . . . is, in fact, many subjects" (p. 200), and
he recognizes "the hopelessness of attempts at coverage" (p. 202).
Nevertheless, his is essentially a monistic view, which presumes that
there are good and bad programs, right and wrong teaching procedures, and a definable set of skills which can be developed and
tested.

Opposed to him are the pluralists, who are more impressed
than he by the amplitude of English and the difficulty of containing
it. "In an acknowledged discipline," wrote William Randel in
1958 (p. 360), "there is general consistency. English is prodigal,
extravagant, inconsistent internally and externally." Many of today's
teachers are not at all sure that they know how to define "the skills
that are really needed by the student of literature and language" (to
quote Booth, 1965, once again), and they doubt that any one program, no matter how carefully devised, will inevitably lead to the
acquisition of those skills. They are therefore more tolerant of variety
and more inclined to leave the selection of courses to the individual
student and his counselor. Nowadays they may also be influenced
by the students' increasing insistence on their right to be consulted
in the planning of their own education. Finally, these teachers are
not as deeply disturbed as Booth by what he calls "the scandal
of determining completion of the major by an adding machine."
They know that the course of studies which constitutes the major
must be of limited duration, and they are aware that its duration
is most conveniently defined in terms of credit hours. But they do

not suppose that they are turning out a finished product, and therefore the totting up of credits is, for them, merely an artificial
formality, about which it is to become exercised.

In 1963 Tuttle and O'Leary (pp. 38, 60) noted, with appro-
bation, a trend "generally in the direction of more requirements and
fewer electives," a tendency toward "greater specificity" in defining
the contents of the major. In 1967 over 75 percent of all departments still retained some requirements for the major, but more and
more of them are beginning to relax their requirements, and the
pluralistic view of programs for the major will eventually prevail.
Two examples will illustrate this trend toward liberalization and
greater permissiveness. For many years previous to 1966 the English
department at Brown University had required all its majors to take
five one-semester period courses *in chronological order*. By this
means the department assured itself that none of its majors would
graduate without some knowledge of the principal episodes in the
history of English literature. This plan was scrapped in 1966,
however, because it was found to be no longer feasible (too much
had to be packed into some of the courses) and because students
were demanding a greater freedom of choice (in particular, they
wanted to take more genre courses). Under the new program English majors at Brown were required to take eight one-semester
courses (in addition to an introductory course in critical reading),
and the department stipulated only that two of them must be in
literature before 1700 and one must be in American literature before
1914. In the spring of 1969, during the brief tenure of President
Ray L. Heffner (himself an English teacher by profession), Brown
revised its general curriculum and its academic policies to permit
its students almost total freedom of choice. The English department
at Stanford revised its program in similar fashion in 1967. It had
formerly required three survey courses, and this number was reduced
to one; several other options were also introduced. A statement
the department's Curriculum Committee, submitted when the new
plan was introduced, succinctly expressed the concept of the major
which prompted the change:

The new proposal continues to recognize a basically historical organi-

zation of courses and provides that all periods be represented in a
student's program. It does, however, steer a middle course between the
present highly prescriptive major and one without specific require-
ments. . . . We think that [the student] and his adviser should have
greater latitude than the present curriculum allows. The heart of the
English major, we believe, is literary experience, not a specific body
of knowledge per se. For this reason we try to allow genuine freedom
of choice as it affects any specific course, while maintaining a general
pattern of historical representation.

Increasing critical sophistication, which leads to increasing uncertainty about just how the history of English literature should be
construed and taught (Was there, for example, a "Romantic
period"?); increasing reluctance to impose an official view of the
subject on their students; increasing inclination to encourage
individual exploration—these and other motives have persuaded
several departments to reconsider their programs for the major and
to redesign them to permit wider latitude. Most important, these
departments share the conviction that "the heart of the English
major. . . is literary experience, not a specific body of knowledge,"
and they are determined not to erect artificial barriers to that experience.

Meanwhile, most of them continue to prescribe at least part
of their programs. The percentage of departments requiring courses
of each type is as follows: survey (74.8 percent); individual authors
(69); American literature (62); linguistics (39); period courses
(39); advanced composition (29); British literature before 1600
(28); literary criticism (25.5); genre course (22.1); other (35.7).
These figures do not vary greatly with the size and type of institution; for example, about the same number of small schools as large
require their English majors to take courses in American literature.
But how little agreement there is on just *which* courses should be
prescribed is revealed by the size of these percentages. It is true that
from 62 to 75 percent of all departments agree that the program for
the major should include one or more survey courses, courses in
individual authors (including Shakespeare), and courses in American literature; but beyond that there is little or no consensus. Only
39 percent require courses in linguistics or the history of the lan-

guage, only 28 percent prescribe courses in early British literature, and so on. It is not that departments have abandoned all requirements for the major but that they have very different notions about which courses are essential to an adequate program.

I also ascertained how *many* courses of each type are required and at what level. From my statistics on this matter the following generalizations may be derived:

When departments require courses of certain types, they usually require only one term of each type. (The only exception is the survey, at least two terms of which are required by most departments.) My data reveal, for example, that 69 percent of all departments require the separate study of individual authors, but almost two thirds of those that do so prescribe only one such course (usually the course in Shakespeare). The number of electives most frequently required is six.

Most departments *do* stipulate when the courses they require should be taken; but, except for the survey (which is usually required in the sophomore year), there is little agreement among them as to which courses should be taken when. About 30 percent of those requiring a course in linguistics, for example, insist that it be taken in the major's junior year; another 25 percent prescribe the senior year, and yet another 45 percent say it may be taken any time. Wayne Booth (1965, p. 214) asserts, with enviable confidence, that "nobody has ever seriously doubted that we learn best when the hurdles to be leapt are placed in some sort of reasonable order," but even he must admit, a few pages later (p. 216), that because "our waters are murky . . . we can hope only to develop a variety of sequences that make sense in different settings." Apparently that is just what departments throughout the nation have been doing for many years. Some are convinced that the course in Shakespeare should be taken early in the major's career, immediately after he has learned to read with critical insight; others believe in reserving the best for the last and therefore have their majors take their Shakespeare in their senior year. Good arguments can be advanced for both procedures, and it is difficult to see that one sequence makes better sense than the other. *If* it were possible to define the educational experience afforded by each course (and to each student) and *if* it were known which sequence of experiences would inevitably conduct students to the competence and knowledge an English major should have (and if *those* virtues could be defined), it would no doubt be possible to design an ideal program which all good departments should adopt. But every one of these matters is murky indeed, so murky as to be almost unfathomable; therefore, departments can do little more than "place the hurdles" in an order that seems reasonable to them and proper for their students. When he describes an actual program which meets his own specifications, Booth tells us that it includes the study of "English literature from 1600 to 1830," to which he quickly adds, "The sequence *could* cover any historical period, short or long, or it could deal with the major writers of all periods, or indeed with any reasonable pattern of types or authors or periods or problems." If the choice of courses to be required is as arbitrary as this statement implies, it is no wonder that departments choose so variously.

Courses for Sophomores Who Plan to Major in English

It is only with regard to sophomores who intend to specialize in English that departments approach something like consensus: 78.6 percent of them continue to hold that, having emerged from freshman English (which usually includes an introduction to the critical reading of literature), students who are headed for the major in English should begin to acquire a summary knowledge of the history of literature. Only 6.4 percent are opposed to such generalized study, 9 percent want their sophomores to combine generalized and specialized study, and 5.5 percent make other suggestions. It is clear, then, that the survey of English literature— which may be the most difficult of all English courses to teach well —remains a staple of the undergraduate curriculum: 78.4 percent of departments offer it; 59.6 commend it to prospective majors. Its worth and even its validity have been debated for decades. "Those who hold that the historical survey has no place in the sophomore course offer two reasons for their belief," wrote Harlan W. Hamilton in 1954 (p. 342). "They argue that the survey is superficial and that it is too much concerned with nonliterary matters." They may also argue, as I would, that it misrepresents the literature by offering students only selections or snippets and that it kills their appetite for rigorous, intensive historical study by presenting over-simplified and canned interpretations of literary history. In response to these objections many departments have modified their survey courses to permit more intensive discussion of certain key works. Hoyt Trowbridge (1965, p. 45) attributes this trend to the influence of the New Criticism.

I. A. Richards suggested in Practical Criticism *that some of the time devoted to extensive reading might profitably be made available for direct training in literary interpretation. Whether influenced by Richards or by their own experience in teaching, many departments of English in American colleges have made room for such training within the traditional survey course by shortening its chronological scope, limiting the works studied chiefly to those by major authors, or otherwise reducing the total amount of material to be covered.*

The logical conclusion to this reform is to convert the survey into a course in masterworks; and, as we have seen, 26.1 percent of all departments have done just that. Others have tried to improve the historical survey in other ways. At the University of Virginia supplementary courses in the works of individual authors or in single recurrent themes are designed to enable majors to study in depth what the survey course has touched on briefly. And at Wellesley College the survey has been replaced by a genre course, Poetry in Three Ages: Renaissance, Neo-Classic, and Romantic, with the proviso that "this course should be fully committed to teaching historical perspective as well as close reading." This change was made, principally, because many Wellesley students had complained that they were required to devote too much of their programs to elementary and cursory studies; they wanted to proceed more rapidly to more challenging studies of problems in literary history and of the works of individual authors. English majors throughout the country expressed the same inclination in interviews. Properly skeptical of the validity of generalizations handed them in the survey course, they asked for more opportunities to derive their own interpretations directly from primary materials—even if this meant that they must remain ignorant of whole periods or bodies of literature.

A new breed of students, whose motives for majoring in English include an almost compulsive desire to find meaning *for* themselves and *by* themselves, may persuade more and more departments to reconsider the value of the one course they now consider all but indispensable.

Tuttle and O'Leary found in 1963 that about 17 percent of the English major's total program, throughout his four years as an undergraduate, was devoted to English. The figure has not changed much in succeeding years. At institutions which have the semester calendar (77.5 percent) and at which students normally take five courses each term, a total of 120 credits is usually required for graduation. The average number of credit hours in English above the freshman level required for the major at these schools is twenty-nine. If six credits for freshman English are added, the total comes to thirty-five, or about 29 percent of the full quota required for graduation. An average of 42.1 credits in English is required for the major at schools which have the quarter calendar, and an average of 28.3 at those which have the trimester calendar. It would require an elaborate computation of evidence difficult to quantify to answer that most important question, "How much of his total academic life does the junior or senior majoring in English devote to his field of concentration?" The total amount might exceed 70 percent. The program for the major in English at the University of Kentucky is typical of many. That institution has the semester calendar, and students normally carry a course load of fifteen hours per term. To graduate as majors in English they must complete eight courses and acquire twenty-four credits in their field of concentration. The following courses are required (percentages indicate how many departments of all sizes and kinds require courses of the kind Kentucky prescribes and thus how common its requirements are): two one-term courses in the survey of English literature (74.8 percent); one one-term course in the works of an individual author (69); one one-term course in American literature (62); one one-term genre course (22.1); three one-term elective courses (82.4). This set of minimum requirements may be considered a norm if it be remembered that there is little normalcy among programs for the major in English.

But these are minimum requirements, and most majors take

more than the minimum. At Swarthmore, for example, a minimum
of eight courses is required, but many students take twelve; at Oberlin thirty-six credits are required, but many accumulate forty-two.
Fearing that some undergraduates, if given perfect freedom of
choice, might devote too much of their total programs to English
and thus neglect their general education, over a third of all departments (34.9 percent) prescribe a maximum number of courses in
English which majors may take. Of those which set such limits about
a third will not permit more than twelve courses, about a quarter
permit no more than fourteen, about 30 percent permit no more
than sixteen, and about 7 percent set some other maximum number.
At Swarthmore the maximum allowed is thirteen courses; at Oberlin
the major may proceed to take courses in excess of the thirty-six
credits required only after he has acquired the 120 credits needed
for graduation, and then the limit is forty-five credits in his field of
concentration. Often these restrictions are prescribed by the college
as a whole; sometimes they are imposed by the department itself. In
every case they are designed (like the provision for "pass/fail"
courses, which has recently become so popular) to encourage the
student to venture outside his area of greatest interest and competence and thus to discourage overspecialization.

Many departments are sensitive to the charge that their
programs for the major violate the principles of liberal education
by demanding too much specialized study. Among those who have
made this accusation is Harold Martin, one of the profession's
ablest critics because he was one of its most distinguished members
before he became president of Union College. Addressing a meeting
of department chairmen, Martin (1967, p. 19) asked them to
imagine a hypothetical situation:

*Consider for a moment what an English department's "principal con-
cerns" would be if no one were needed to teach English. What would
be left of the present undergraduate major or of graduate study? The
question is entirely serious, and any serious answer, I think, will reveal
at least that professionalism—specialism, willy-nilly—now dominates
both. English departments prize most those students who most hand-
somely fulfill professional expectations. . . . It is senseless, I think, to
quarrel with the logic of this patronage, but it is also foolish to overlook
the premises for it. The truth is that English teachers, for school and*

college, are needed, and English departments feel an obligation to produce them. The "primary concerns" of their major and graduate programs are to do exactly that.

To this indictment the departments might respond, first, that they do not deliberately and formally distinguish between undergraduates who plan to become college teachers (that is, those who intend to go on to graduate work) and those who do not; 75.9 percent of all departments say they make no such distinction, and 70.3 percent say that the need to prepare some students for graduate work does *not* influence their programs for the major in any significant way. Those departments which do identify majors who plan to enter graduate school usually offer them special counseling and little more. Only 12.1 percent of all departments offer special courses designed to prepare students for graduate work; only 6.3 percent provide special tracks of regular courses. This is the extent to which the need to coach such students influences undergraduate programs directly. Furthermore, the number of majors who actually go to graduate school is so small that the "primary concern" of English departments *cannot* be to produce college teachers of English. Throughout the nation the average percentage of English majors who subsequently do graduate work in this field is 24.9. In other words, only a quarter of all students who major in English are inspired to become college teachers of that subject. The chairman of the English department at one prestigious eastern university summed up his opinions this way: "If our four or five best majors each year enrolled in our graduate program, we would *really* have a fine program. But they don't. Most of them go into law or medicine, and I'm glad they do. We want to do more than reproduce our own kind."

Finally, departments might point out that it is very difficult to define and to measure overspecialization. Is the teacher overspecializing when he devotes three class periods to a single scene in Shakespeare? Obviously the answer depends on how much meaning he can find in the text and what kinds of meaning he reveals to his students. The very titles of some undergraduate courses offered by some departments (especially those at very large universities) may seem prima facie evidence of excessive specialization: thus, the department at the University of Illinois lists Spenser and His Con-

temporaries, Mark Twain and the Rise of Realism, and Popular
Ballads and Folk Songs in the United States. But the study of any
one of these subjects *may* lead to discussion of fundamental, universal issues rather than to mere professionalism or pedantry.
Furthermore, courses of this kind account for only a very small
portion of the total effort devoted to the major. Illinois has about
410 majors in English (and 550 teacher-training majors), but the
average annual enrollment in each of these courses is about sixteen.
As reported earlier, a majority of departments (53.4 percent) now
look for teachers of general ability, not for specialists, when they
recruit new members; and many instructors, once they are hired,
are invited or required to teach courses well outside their areas of
graduate specialization. These and other circumstances may help to
prevent overspecialization, which most English teachers would
probably condemn as heartily as their critics—if only they could be
sure just what it is.

Foreign-Language Requirements

Students who major in English must meet foreign-language
requirements at 81.4 percent of all colleges and universities. (The
number may be declining: several institutions, including Michigan
State University, have recently abolished their language requirements.) At about two thirds of these institutions the requirements
are college-wide or the same for all majors; at the rest they are
prescribed by the English department for its majors alone. The
most common requirement is two years of college work in a single
foreign language or the equivalent of such work. It appears that
sectarian schools are most likely to require command of a foreign
language and that schools in the South Central and North Atlantic
sections of the nation are more likely than others to do so. Most
departments justify their requirements on the ground that familiarity
with a foreign language will enhance the student's sensitivity to his
own language, not on the ground that he needs to be prepared to
read foreign texts in the original.

The Senior Thesis

The question of whether all majors in English should be
required to write a lengthy essay or undergraduate thesis before they
graduate is answered *for* departments at most large institutions:

they *cannot* maintain such a requirement, because they have too many majors and not enough teachers to direct and read the theses. Only 2.4 percent of departments in large schools require a thesis, only 10.5 percent of those in medium-sized schools, and only 12.4 percent of those in small schools. These figures are bound to prove distressing to Wayne Booth (1965, p. 210), who sees the senior thesis as "the most important achievement" in the major's undergraduate career. In the course of defending this requirement he rehearses the two most common arugments against it (p. 216): that "teachers just don't have time to supervise such work" and that "students are not up to it." To the first he answers, "Why do the over-worked departments find it impossible to turn over some of the responsibility to the students? Why not cancel half of the required coursework and use the saving in staff time to provide supervision for independent projects?" To the second, "If four years of course-work, two of them primarily under the English department, do not produce students who are able to approach a literary or linguistic problem on their own and write a literate account of their conclu-sions, then surely the answer is not to dodge the embarrassing test of our failure but rather to consider the causes and remove them."

But there is another fact, which Booth does not seriously consider: that many undergraduates—including some of the most competent—are simply not ready to make an extended statement, even when they reach their senior year. For many of them further coursework, demanding as it usually does a number of shorter papers, may have greater educational benefit than the struggle to eke out a thesis (a struggle sometimes won only by their faculty advisor's lending undue assistance—in effect, writing the thesis with them). For the student who happens to find just the right topic—one that engages his strongest interests and enables him to collect and relate much of what he has learned—the senior thesis may in-deed prove a dramatic conclusion to four years of college work. But for most others it becomes just another chore, just another arti-ficial hurdle to be cleared. Several departments with graduate pro-grams in English (notably those at Rutgers and at Johns Hopkins) have recently revised their programs for the Ph.D. to permit candi-dates to submit a collection of essays in lieu of the traditional doctoral dissertation; others may wish to follow their example at the undergraduate level by modifying their regulation that all English majors must write a senior thesis.

Independent Study

It was about fifteen years ago that colleges began to see that they might allow some students to learn by themselves, with little faculty guidance. Now 73.1 percent make some provision for independent study. (That figure is slightly higher for large schools than for small, lowest for medium-sized schools.) Only a very few (2.1 percent) require independent study of all majors, but many encourage them to undertake it. The most common practice is simply to announce that independent study is available to those who qualify for it (and who can persuade faculty members to supervise their projects); about one third of all departments follow this procedure. Another quarter reserve independent study for honors students, and the rest provide for it in other ways.

Many departments have instituted independent study programs in the hope that they might alleviate the faculty's teaching load and thus allow it to improve its other programs. But this seldom occurs. At institutions where independent study has become popular, it has often proved very costly of faculty time and energies. A member of the English department at Colby College recently asserted that "the most expensive program we ever devised is independent study." The reason seems to be that such study can never be wholly independent and that students who are granted this privilege often become as dependent as tutees, demanding a great deal of individual attention. If twenty students are permitted to study independently, one less class may be needed. But the department may find to its dismay that it has, in effect, assumed the burden of twenty tutorials.

Moreover, the feasibility and educational value of independent study have been questioned by some departments that have tried it. In 1966 the English department at Wellesley College revised its plan for the major to include six weeks of independent study in the junior year. Its aim was to urge its highly competent students to pursue their own interests and to make their own discoveries. Two years later the department was forced to admit that very few majors were making good use of the time set aside for independent study. Wellesley's experience confirms what others have found: that, for those rare students whose curiosity has led them into realms not covered by the regular curriculum, independent study may be wholly appropriate, almost necessary (and therefore some provision for it should certainly be made), but that to require it of all students is probably a mistake.

Courses for Seniors

A small number of departments (5.7 percent of the total) provide special courses which are required of all seniors majoring in English. Indiana's catalog description of its "senior seminars" characterizes most of these culminating courses: each seminar is devoted to "a thorough study of one or more major British or American writers or of one significant theme in English and American literature." The primary purpose of these courses is not to "fill gaps" but to ensure that all majors will have some experience of intensive study before they graduate. Students of English at Yale, for example, are likely to find themselves in large classes during their sophomore and junior years, but to complete the program for the major they must take a full year of "discussion courses," each of which has a limited focus and a limited enrollment. At Swarthmore two seminars of this kind—one in Shakespeare and the other in Problems of Literary Study—are prescribed for seniors in the regular program. The "problems" which may be addressed in the latter are so numerous that the course may be used as a testing ground for innovations in teaching or for new explorations of old subject matter. Most departments would like to leave some room in their curriculum for such experimentation, and senior seminars of this kind (like the freshman seminars described earlier) may serve the double function of encouraging fresh teaching and of affording majors a final chance to study in depth.

The Comprehensive Examination

"Why, they could graduate as majors in English without having *heard* of 'In Memoriam,' or the pathetic fallacy, or Adelaide Crapsey!" Sooner or later this lament, or some version of it, is heard whenever departments meet to discuss the adequacy of their programs for the major. It is a source of great concern to some members of the profession that every year degrees are awarded to students whose knowledge of English and American literature remains sadly imperfect despite the eight or ten courses each has taken as a major in this field. Some device must be found, these teachers feel, to certify the major's command of his discipline, and no device seems more logical than a comprehensive examination which will test both his erudition and his competence as a critic. According to Wayne Booth (1965, p. 206), this final trial should elicit from the student "one supreme effort" and should not only prove his right to the degree but should also prevent "the anticlimax experienced by the student who simply completes the right number of courses."

It would appear, however, that the great majority of departments throughout the nation either cannot or will not institute such an examination. Only 25.3 percent of all departments now require the comprehensive, and most of these are at small schools. Just as they are unable, for lack of manpower, to supervise and to evaluate the large number of senior theses their majors would produce if each were required to write one, so departments in large institutions cannot administer a comprehensive examination. A case in point is the department at Cornell, which abandoned this requirement when its corps of majors grew to such size that it became impossible to read the bluebooks they filled; that department now sets a comprehensive examination only for its honor students (and that is of modified form, as explained below). Duke and the University of Nebraska have eliminated the comprehensive for the same reason. Indeed, only 3.4 percent of all English departments with more than 150 majors (at all levels) retain the comprehensive, and one may assume that, for all practical purposes, that number becomes the cutoff point beyond which the requirement is no longer feasible.

At Reed College and a few others the comprehensive is taken in the junior year and becomes a kind of qualifying examination for the major; at the University of Chicago and the University of Virginia majors must take two examinations, a test of factual knowledge in the junior year and a test of critical ability in the senior year. At the great majority of institutions which retain the comprehensive, however, the examination is taken near the end of the student's senior year. In most instances his fellow seniors majoring in other fields must also take comprehensives: the requirement is college-wide at 51 percent of all schools at which it is maintained.

Several departments declare that they continue to require the comprehensive "only because we have to"—that is, because it would be difficult or impossible to persuade the faculty as a whole to abandon the requirement.

A six-hour comprehensive is the most common: 40.6 percent of all comprehensives are of this length, 26.6 percent are of three-hour duration, and 32.8 percent are of some other length. At 57.7 percent of those schools which retain the test, the English department issues a syllabus or list of works to be covered. Usually the lists read much like the tables of contents of the standard anthologies of English and American literature, with whole novels and plays added; some departments merely refer their majors to such anthologies. The examination itself may consist of an "objective" section, designed to test rote knowledge; several "spot passage" or identification questions; and several essay questions, most of which require the student to compare works from different periods and bodies of literature. A few departments substitute the Graduate Record Examination for all or part of their comprehensive. That test, which is graded electronically and is therefore limited to multiple-choice questions, can determine only whether or not the student has the "right" answer; it cannot acknowledge and reward original perception. Its serious inadequacy has been pointed up by Randolph H. Hudson (1969, p. 50): "The multiple-choice test assumes that the important question is *what* is the right answer; whereas the real question is why is one of the answers superior to the others?" In the opinion of some, including myself, the present GRE in English is a caricature of all examinations which attempt to reduce British and American literature to a tidy, testable subject.

In an effort to encourage freer, more direct, and more personal responses to their questions, 9 percent of all departments include an oral examination, usually of one hour. A very few enlist the services of outside examiners, eminent teachers from other schools who visit the host campus for a day or two to examine candidates orally or to read responses to written examinations they have set. Some teachers doubt the value of this (rather costly) procedure, because they observe that the visitors are seldom sure of exactly what the examinees have studied and are therefore unusually lenient out of courtesy and uncertainty. Others—notably faculty members at Swarthmore and the University of Rochester (where the outsiders examine only honors students, it should be said)—are confident that no other method serves the purposes of the comprehensive as well. Students prepare to answer not just the favorite questions of the local faculty but questions any first-rate scholar might ask. This, in turn, frees the faculty from coaching its students for its own examination, with the slight hypocrisy that entails. Furthermore, the students and the faculty have an opportunity to meet and talk with their distinguished guests.

The great value of the comprehensive examination, in the opinion of those who advocate it, is that it encourages (or forces) students to read works not covered in their regular courses, to fill in their knowledge of literary history, and to achieve something like an overview of their subject. If the examination is well planned, it should enable students to draw on the fund of knowledge and insights they have accumulated during their years as majors, to perceive and define interrelationships among disparate or distant works, and thus to transcend the fragmentation resulting from the course system. The department may liberalize its program for the major and permit more options, it is argued, if it can be certain that all its majors must familiarize themselves with the main corpus of British and American literature in preparation for the comprehensive. For these and other reasons some members of the profession continue to endorse this requirement; Wayne Booth (1965, pp. 206, 207) is even willing to say that "the lack of a comprehensive is one of the surest signs of an ill-designed program" and that "almost any comprehensive is better than nothing."

Others are not so sure of the worth of these examinations as testing, much less as educational, devices. They point out that the comprehensive can never be truly comprehensive, because undergraduates cannot—and probably should not—be expected to know all there is to know about their subject. The most that can be demanded of most of them is a superficial knowledge of the principal figures in the history of British and American literature and some ability to find meaning in works they have had time to read and compare. Recognizing this fact, several departments have abandoned all pretense that their final examination is a "comprehensive" and have converted it to a set-book test of critical skills. Thus, candidates for honors at Cornell University take three two-and-a-half-hour examinations, each devoted to a single work which has been identified well in advance. (One year the works consisted of a play by Shakespeare, a poem by Pope, and a novel by George Eliot.) And at Pomona the following announcement was distributed to all majors:

Beginning with the class of 1968, a new type of Comprehensive Examination for English majors will be given. Instead of asking seniors to spend most of their time writing on a large field (i.e., all of English literature) which no one will be able to know thoroughly, students will be offered a choice of special fields which they can know well. The General Reading List is considerably shortened, and special field reading lists will be available for students to choose. In addition, each year a single book, or work of literature, will be set by the department for intensive study.

To redefine the concept of the final examination in this way is not only to acknowledge, once again, the impossibility of containing "English" but also to affirm the department's belief that the ability to discuss a limited topic well is of greater value than the ability to drop names and dates.

Many departments report, however, that even their most carefully designed examinations produce only mediocre results. Each year, they say, they are embarrassed to read the bluebooks of seniors they will soon discharge as certified "experts" in English. And discharge them they will, because almost no one is prevented from graduating by the comprehensive examination. At a majority (54.7 percent) of schools which retain it, the incidence of failure on the comprehensive is less than 4 percent; at several schools no student has failed in many years. Those few who do are usually allowed to take the examination again or to qualify for graduation in some other way. Thus, it could be argued that the comprehensive examination is not only not comprehensive but also not an examination, since it does not discriminate among those who take it.

The English majors themselves are well aware, of course, that they are being asked to take a nontest, to clear a hurdle which trips almost none of the runners, and their somewhat cynical attitude toward the comprehensive may be attributed to their awareness of this fact. "We know we are going to pass," said one senior at

Kenyon. "Any student who gets this far as an English major is bound to pass." This, in turn, may account for the dull, perfunctory answers their teachers must read. No doubt those students who prepare conscientiously for the examination derive educational benefits from this exercise. For too many, however, it becomes merely a final initiation rite, which they suffer because they know it means so little.

Honors Programs

At about two thirds of all colleges and universities the regular program for the major in English is supplemented by an honors program, designed to provide the most capable students with opportunities for more intensive study in close consultation with members of the faculty. Obviously, there is greater need for such programs at large schools than at small, especially if the latter are highly selective; as the chairman at one such college said (with some exaggeration), "*All* our majors are honors students." And in fact the incidence of honors programs does vary greatly with the size of the institution. Eighty percent of large schools offer honors programs of one kind or another, as compared with 75 percent of medium-sized schools and only 54 percent of small schools. Half of these are departmental programs, 27 percent are college-wide programs, and the rest are some combination of both.

Students are selected for most college-wide honors programs in their freshman year, for most departmental programs in their junior year. Admissions procedures and criteria vary greatly from campus to campus; the only evidence used by a majority of departments is the student's grade average (a B average is most commonly required). Sectarian schools have the highest percentage of college-wide honors programs, and most of them admit students in the freshman year; accordingly, these schools place less emphasis on grades, either because they are not available at that point or because they are not significant.

A salutary trend away from selecting honors students merely on the basis of such "objective" evidence as test scores and grades may be observed at several institutions. Thus, a departmental committee charged with reviewing Duke's "special programs in the major" recommended as follows:

Candidates for the Honors Program should not be selected on the basis of quality-point ratio alone. The committee recommends that the Director of Undergraduate Studies, in conference with the tutors, extend invitations to those students who satisfy the university's requirement for admission to an honors program [a B average] and who in their judgment have the ability to complete the program with excellence.

Recommendations and reports from instructors are now given greatest weight by the director and the tutors at Duke. At the University of Connecticut those who administer the college-wide honors program have adopted most of the admissions procedures followed by small, selective colleges—interviews, letters of recommendation, test scores, high school grades, and class standing—to identify the one hundred (out of twenty-five hundred) freshmen who will be admitted to their program. To achieve the purposes of that program, they believe they must find not only "little achievers" but also students who have some originality of mind and an independent enthusiasm for learning.

The programs to which such superior students are admitted are usually distinguished by special courses or special sections of regular courses and special provisions or requirements for the degree. Quite predictably, larger schools, which have greater resources, are more likely than medium-sized or small to offer special instruction for honors students: 82.4 percent of large, 75.9 percent of medium, and only 49.3 percent of small institutions provide such special classes. Among the special provisions or requirements for honors students, the most common is some form of independent study. Fewer large departments than small require independent study; more large departments provide tutorials and demand a thesis and/or a comprehensive examination—all of which suggests that large departments take their honors programs somewhat more seriously than small.

Two thriving honors programs, one offered by a small college and the other by a large university, will serve to illustrate the form such programs may take and the benefits they may afford well-qualified and well-motivated students. At Swarthmore, where 40 percent of the student body is enrolled in honors programs, candidates for honors in English devote as much as half their junior or senior years to special seminars. Four of the six seminars each is permitted to take must be in their major field (and at least one of these must be in Chaucer, Shakespeare, or Milton); two must be in a minor field. Enrollment in each seminar is limited to seven students, and each meets once a week for four and a half hours. Students write a paper every other week for each seminar, but no honors thesis is required. The comprehensive examination for honors students consists of six three-hour tests, one in each of the fields covered by the seminars they have taken. As reported above, these examinations are set (and read) by outsiders, who also conduct a twenty-minute oral examination of each candidate and who decide what honors he will be awarded. Discussions in honors seminars at Swarthmore usually address challenging problems raised by the literature; no time in class is wasted on reviewing basic knowledge. So great is the intellectual energy of these honors candidates that they may be expected to prepare themselves for the intensive explorations to which the seminar meetings are devoted. Thus, the honors program at this college involves something like communal independent study.

Prospective honors students at Cornell University are picked in their sophomore year, when they are assigned to special sections (limited to twenty-five students) of the survey or Great Writers course. In each term of their junior year they enroll in an honors seminar, which constitutes a quarter of their total program. They may choose from a battery of such courses, each of which is of limited focus (some recent titles: The Novel of Manners, The Humanistic Imagination, and Shakespeare and the Critics). Each course is "designed to acquaint the student with the different ways in which literary study may be conducted, with the sort of information one may need in order to appreciate the full import of a particular text, and with some of the value systems that have been applied to literature—in short to show the student how to come to the fullest understanding of a text and how to find the value in the work which the instructor believes the work to have," to quote a departmental announcement. Students are required to write a number of essays, totaling approximately thirty pages for each honors seminar, and the topics for their honors theses (outlined in the spring of their junior year and completed in the fall or winter of their senior year) usually emerge from their work in the seminars. Finally, all must pass the set-book examination described above. The forty to fifty students who graduate from Cornell each year with honors in English have thus been treated to a rich if rigorous series of studies: in addition to their regular coursework, they have participated in small-group discussions (often conducted by senior professors), have written numerous critical papers, have had a tutorial leading to the completion of a lengthy essay, and have proved their ability to read with insight almost any text put in front of them. Departments which can afford programs like Cornell's may be reasonably sure that they have served their best students well.

Of all colleges and universities, 86.2 percent award degrees with honors (variously designated "summa cum laude," "highest honors," "with great distinction," and so forth), but not all which do have honors programs; some give honors to all students who achieve a certain grade-point average in a general program (thus, "honors" means only that students have received especially good grades). At many institutions students who complete departmental honors programs successfully are awarded general honors, at some they are awarded only departmental honors, and at others they receive both. The policy of awarding general honors is most popular at small schools, which offer fewest departmental honors programs. Large public schools, with their many separate programs, are most likely to award departmental honors or both.

TEN

The State of Undergraduate English

"It looks like English remains a large, gray, ramshackle institution." That was the conclusion one member of the survey's advisory committee reached when he had completed his study of my findings—and his description will seem accurate to many. About the size of this institution there can be no dispute; the teaching of English to undergraduates is surely one of the two or three largest enterprises in American higher education, and although its great bulk will certainly shrink if all liberal education is starved in the years ahead, much of English will probably survive. Its special monopoly on language and literature will sustain it despite its obvious infirmities.

To some members of the profession those infirmities seem

embarrassingly obvious; as they contemplate the edifice which is undergraduate English today, they find it gray indeed and badly in need of repair. In particular, they are struck by the fact (which some of my statistics may be used to confirm) that few if any *major* renovations in its structure have been effected in the past two or three decades. Of all departments polled by my survey, 87 percent said that they had recently changed their programs for undergraduates or had introduced innovations (61.8 percent had altered their freshman programs, 44 percent had revised their general curriculums, and 30.5 percent had changed their programs for the major); but close examination of the changes reported reveals that most of them were minor adjustments, reshufflings of familiar offerings, or experiments which had been tried and abandoned elsewhere. There are few earlier statistics to compare with those I gathered, and therefore I cannot verify or disprove the common suspicion that English programs have remained almost static over the past twenty years. But the very fact that I was able to classify about 80 percent of the courses now being offered as versions of types which have been standard for decades suggests that that suspicion is well founded. Courses in black literature, in "women's studies," and in the film may be the only important recent additions to the conventional curriculum, and the vogue for black literature seems to be on the wane. Almost all the rest have been around for many years, and that in itself seems damning evidence to some critics of the profession.

Others are not surprised that catalog descriptions look much the same today as they did in the thirties and forties. They observe that this profession serves as custodian of the literature of the past, a more or less stable corpus which is best served to students in the portions which compose the conventional curriculum. Even those departments that have designed their programs from scratch, they note, include courses of several common types: thus, the catalog of Simon Fraser University in British Columbia and of the University of California, Santa Cruz—both new institutions passionately dedicated to innovation—list courses entitled Shakespeare and The Romantics. If the course in Shakespeare is now being taught at those universities—or anywhere else—just as it was taught in the

1930s, that were stagnation indeed. It seems probable, however, that many of those who are now conducting this inevitable course are offering students a brand of Shakespeare which differs from older readings of his works as Kott differs from Bradley. And it is surely not the age of the bottles but the character of the wine they contain which one must judge as one seeks to evaluate current programs in English.

Nevertheless, there is a great *yearning* for change among college teachers of English throughout the land. Whether it is because they were trained as critics or because the nature of their discipline all but precludes their producing quantifiable evidences of success or failure, the members of this profession are a self-critical, uncertain lot, who continually suppose, most of them, that there *must* be other, better ways to accomplish their aims. As I traveled about the country conducting interviews for this survey, I was impressed by the fact that those I talked to were often more eager to hear the news from abroad—especially if it were news of innovation —than they were to tell me about their own programs. I encountered very little complacency and many expressions of an almost desperate craving for word of new courses, new programs, new administrative procedures. The public demonstrations of student discontent which have occurred since my interviews can only have intensified that craving.

In their dissatisfaction with what they are now doing and in their nearly frantic efforts to conceive new programs suitable to the disposition of their students and to the tenor of the times, English teachers find they must once again confront and seek solutions to certain large problems which have plagued the profession ever since it reached its maturity early in the century. My extensive examination of the profession's present practices and my discussions with hundreds of its members lead me to conclude that most of these problems can be reduced to three major questions or concerns, all of which overlap and are interrelated: how to reconcile institutional procedures with the teaching of a subject that is largely inimical to institutions; how to determine what constitutes good teaching of English; how to define and defend English as a discipline. To review the specific forms in which these hoary questions arise for today's departments and their members is to describe the present state of undergraduate English.

English and the Institution

As he walks into Section L27 of English 239B (Contemporary Drama) to deliver his fifty-minute lecture on the Theatre of the Absurd to students 110578, 234690, 403921 and so on, Payroll Number 6954021 may note a certain absurdity in his own position, may wonder if these are precisely the right circumstances under which to represent a literature that makes a mock of institutions. As he plans his syllabus for the course in the novel, he may perceive an irony in teaching *Hard Times* by modern versions of Gradgrind's methods. Or as he offers his orderly explication of Herrick's "Delight in Disorder," he may ask himself whether the institutional procedures to which he is committed and the critical practices they encourage are likely to engender delight of any kind. The English teacher is a man divided. He has a double commitment, and often his twin loyalties seem incompatible. On the one hand, he presents himself to his students as a partisan of literature, a defender of the humane values it expresses, and an enemy of all that inhibits the free exercise of the individual imagination. Like the literature which sustains him, he is pro-Sleary and anti-Gradgrind. On the other hand, he is an officer of an institution, and he makes his living by subscribing to the proposition, fundamental to all institutional operations, that men can collaborate effectively only if they standardize their procedures, objectify their judgments, and impose regularity on human behavior. The institution insists on definition, on consistency, on system. It likes "behavioral objectives" and quantifiable achievements. The literature resists all that. At its best it testifies to the enormous variety and versatility of the human mind.

Of course, there are always members of the profession—usually called "good administrators"—who are willing to ignore this discrepancy between the spirit of the literature and the means by which it is purveyed; they are the men who want uniformity and predictability, who like to measure and certify, who conceive of education as the orderly production of graduates, not as the lucky coincidence of mind with mind. But there are others, most of them to be found among those younger members of the profession who have not been overly impressed by the programs of graduate studies to which they have been subjected, who live daily with their inability to reconcile their delight in the materials they are privileged to teach with their distaste for the standardization many departments—particularly those in large institutions—find it proper to demand. These ambivalents are the heirs to the humanist tradition, and to them it is an abiding irony that so much of undergraduate English in America today looks very like a bad poem: derivative, factitious, and regular only for the sake of completing its own form.

Recent efforts to liberalize academic procedures and to approach something like "controlled anarchy" in institutions of higher learning may represent responses not only to students' demands for greater freedom but also to their teachers' awareness of the absurdity lurking in any attempt to regiment liberal education. One may be moved to abolish grades, for example, not only because students resent being rated but also because the grades imply absolute judgments good teachers of humane subjects know they cannot make. Similarly, the elimination of requirements—say, those for the major in English—may represent not only a concession to rebellious students but also a recognition of diversity and of the need to live with a pluralistic view of the educational process. Other contemporary events—the abolition of common examinations, the decline of the omnibus textbook, and the growing popularity of the "clustered" university—can also be seen as expressions of a discontent with the systematized teaching of nonsytematic matter. The first impulse of those who are now concerned to protect the humanities from excessive regimentation seems to be not to replace existing institutional structures but to decentralize, to refract, to decompose them. Even older, more conservative members of the profession are being moved in increasing numbers to support the redefinition or abolition of academic regulations in the hope that some artificial barriers to teaching and learning may be eliminated.

Quality of Instruction

As I have noted earlier, college teaching is a curious profession in that it continually subjects its members to review and ranking but has little evidence on which to judge them and no well-defined standards of excellence. Even small, intimate departments cannot determine with any assurance the quality of instruction they offer their students. And, in this case, what cannot be measured in miniature cannot be measured at large: no grand survey can ascertain exactly how well college English is being taught throughout the land. We now know that some 1200 departments conduct courses in American literature, but just how Emerson is faring this week in Florida, in Missouri, and in Oregon no one—not even those who teach him—can presume to say. We can, however, point to certain trends in undergraduate English, and we can speculate on how recent shifts in attitude, policy, and practice may be influencing the quality of teaching.

One such trend, evident in almost every sector I surveyed, is toward a greater regard for individuality and for personality. All of a piece with the movement toward disintegrating institutions, this welcome trend is away from wholesale instruction toward multiform programs designed to respect singularity and to encourage direct communication between teacher and student, student and book. It takes many forms: seminars for freshmen and sophomores, tutorials for upper-division students, independent study programs, special topics courses, special programs and provisions for minority groups, honors programs, "inner colleges," additional counseling facilities. Even very large universities are adopting these and other means to accommodate the diverse preferences of their students and to re-establish personal contact among members of the academic community. For years English departments have sustained a program which still offers many American undergraduates their *only* opportunity to experience such contact: freshman English. Now they and their colleagues in other departments seem determined to do at all levels what English teachers have long been doing for freshmen. The motives underlying this determination may be more or less laudable. Some teachers fear student revolt. Some share the students' aversion to bigness and the anonymity it imposes; administrators and faculty members yearn as the students do for intellectual fellowship in a divisive world. Others are moved by a growing uncertainty that they know what is right for all students. To them it seems arrogant to prescribe for students in the mass when teachers disagree and are unsure of their own values. In a time of general skepticism and unrest, individualized communication, with all its cost and inefficiency, seems especially precious, even essential.

Consistent with this impulse toward atomizing institutions and toward respecting the uniqueness of each student is a view of teaching which, if not radically new, has recently become more widely endorsed. F. Parvin Sharpless summarized this concept when, in 1967, he reported his response to the collection of essays entitled *The College Teaching of English*. In the course of deploring much of what he found there, Sharpless had occasion to distinguish between a traditional view of teaching and what he called "a kind of existential pedagogy." He characterized (p. 34) the latter as assuming that

to learn is to develop, to become, to fulfill one's potential, and the means to these ends are not discipline and restraint, but freedom, encouragement, love. Under these terms the teacher neither lectures nor prescribes, because his "truth" is experiential, growing out of situation and context, out of the crossing in time of teacher, student, and work of art. In his students and in himself he values originality, imagination, and evidence of growth. In the classroom he values engagement; his aim is to unsettle the perceptual pattern of the student, but not to prescribe a new one. In his teaching he may discard all lecture notes or prepared outlines, coming to class with a detailed grasp of the work at hand, derived from a fresh study of it, and with his intellect and sensibilities open and receptive to what will happen. He considers that only when students are involved in a kind of spontaneous excitement of learning will the class justify itself.

It is unfortunate that many of the phrases Sharpless was forced to use in his effort to identify this position—phrases like "to fulfill one's potential," "evidence of growth," and "spontaneous excitement of learning"—have now become clichés, unfortunate because their familiarity may distract us from the import of what is being defined. If this view of teaching were generally adopted—and recent evidence suggests that more and more teachers are finding it congenial —much of undergraduate English might be transformed. Courses and curriculums might be redesigned, examinations and grades might be abolished, and, most important, the daily conduct of classes might be liberalized to encourage more "spontaneous excitement." The fact that some of these reforms have already been

effected by individual teachers, departments, and whole colleges
attests to the popularity of the cluster of attitudes Sharpless has
defined.

Reaction against those attitudes and the practices they in-
spire has set in at some institutions, where a fear of chaos (and of
political reprisals) has moved authorities to reinstate absolute requirements and to impose other controls on teaching and learning.
But the general drift of our culture is surely away from absolutism
of every kind, and the temper of today's students, with their passion
for direct experience, seems certain to thwart any effort to return
to merely traditional pedagogy. Sharpless (1967, p. 34) concedes
that in the new pedagogy "there is a Faustian temptation to ego
and vanity, which may lead to error and which will divorce [the
teacher] from the minds of others and isolate him inside his self-
consciousness." One might add that the cult of immediacy may blind
teachers and students to everything that is not present and easily
seized. But safeguards against these pitfalls can be installed in almost
any course. The man who teaches modern literature, for example,
can see to it that many voices, including appropriate voices from the
past, are heard in his classroom and can insist that his subject be
"engaged" in its full complexity. If what Albert Marckwardt has
called the new "emphasis on experience and involvement," and
Arthur Eastman the "preference for power rather than knowledge,
for experience rather than information, for engagement rather than
criticism," become nothing more than faddish professional mannerisms, they will leave undergraduate English untouched. But if
they are expressions of deep conviction and a genuine concern for
English, they will affect it profoundly—and probably for the better.

Vulnerability of English

Meanwhile, departments of English find themselves in a
paradoxical position. As I have reported, many have succeeded
during the last two decades in divesting themselves of service obligations (including, in a small but growing number of cases, freshman
composition) and have moved toward consolidating their domains,
delimiting their functions, and defining their discipline. It is now
possible to say, for example, that, whatever English departments
are supposed to do, it does not include teaching oratory and certain

kinds of commercial writing. But all the while they have been struggling to reassert their integrity, these departments have been subjected to new influences and demands, with the result that the question "What is English?" has never been more urgent than it is today or more difficult to answer.

As posed by some critics of the profession, both inside and outside its ranks, that question quickly becomes "What does the study of English have to do with the rest of modern life?" Simply to say that it is *part* of modern life—one of many discrete and legitimate intellectual activities in which men may engage—does not satisfy such critics. They want assurance that English is conceived and practiced not as an autotelic discipline but as a means of comprehending, of controlling, and thus of enhancing life *beyond* the printed page. Language is a medium, they continually remind us, and literature is a representation of human experience. To study either as if it were a mere artifact—"a fascinating clockworks that [tells] no time," in Benjamin DeMott's clever phrase—is to neglect what the medium conveys and to ignore what the literature represents. And in the opinion of these critics English teachers are often guilty of just that. DeMott himself (1969, p. 143) makes this charge: "I believe the English teacher isn't usually and primarily engaged in the activity of encouraging students to find the bearing of this book and that poem and this "composition" on their own lives. . . . I believe the English teacher is inhibited about giving himself to the labor of drawing men into an effort to reflect upon and understand their own experience."

Now, the complaint that English has been "emptied of content" and has become "an enclosed, sealed-off enterprise, locked into terms of discourse which . . . are too unrelenting, self-referring to be worth praise" is not new. As Richard Ellmann has said in response to DeMott's attack (*Newsweek,* October 13, 1969, p. 72), "We know that every twenty years there has to be this crying out." Indeed, it might be revealing to make a historical study of the criticism DeMott is the latest to revive. Perhaps it could be determined that English is always accused of parochialism, of abdicating its responsibilities to the humanities, and of neglecting "life" when life in the nation becomes especially confused and frightening. Certainly English is unusually vulnerable to such criticism. It is, as I have said, the one discipline which has something all others must use; therefore, it is everyone's property and everyone's concern. And when modern men feel an urgent need for enlightenment or simply for some expression of matters that trouble them, they often turn to literature as men of an earlier age turned to religion. If they then find, or think they find, the priests of English hoarding the sacred texts and practicing arcane critical rites, their resentment will be great—and perhaps justified.

In 1969 and 1970 some such resentment coincided with widespread demands for social reforms, and this has intensified the pressures on English. Because of the exigencies of the times, it is now argued, English teachers can no longer be permitted the luxury of teaching language as language and literature as literature; instead, they must contribute in every way they can to the amelioration of social conditions. Linguists must work to combat false concepts of dialect and the injustices those concepts engender; black literature must be taught to "sensitize" students and thus to improve racial relations; courses in urban literature must be offered to illuminate the problems of the cities. No opportunity to "politicize" English and to relate it to the social concerns of the days should be overlooked. Those who take this position insist that teaching is a political act, whether or not it is intended to be: to read a poem one way—say, with attention to structure and the interaction of words—is not to read it another way and perhaps to be guilty of complacency or indifference to human suffering. Simply to take delight in aesthetic success seems to them an aristocratic, belletristic indulgence.

Two objections to this argument may be raised: the first is that it treats literature almost exclusively as document and assumes, quite naïvely, that social therapy can be effected simply by confronting students with the right documents, properly interpreted. But such indoctrination may offend as often as it persuades, and it reduces education to the acquisition of social attitudes deemed "correct" by official interpretors. The second objection follows from this: it is that to limit English to the study of documents pertinent to today's social problems would be to impoverish the discipline while pretending to enrich it. At present English teachers and their students can do many things, from analyzing language to exploring the relation of literature to life. Not everything they do will prepare them in any easily discernible way for enlightened social action. But even their most bookish activities—disentangling a metaphor, for example, or clarifying an episode in literary history—may help to develop powers of discrimination and critical habits of mind which are needed today just as much as mere awareness of injustice. Those who would convert English into courses in current events would deny its riches—which, though they have always embarrassed it, have always given it strength.

"Why should things—objects, feelings, situations—not stand in better with English teachers than they do?" asks Benjamin DeMott (1969, p. 152). The answer, of course, is that English teachers are on the side both of things and of the words that represent them. Their office is to mediate between words and things and to teach students not to confuse the two. The future of English will depend not on how many things can be brought into the classroom but on how many fine minds can be enlisted to serve as equilibrists between words and things, between the past and the present, between reading about life and living it.

APPENDIX

A Checklist for Departments

Following are some questions departments may wish to put to themselves as they review their operations and their programs for undergraduates. This list is not exhaustive, but it does touch on many matters I have found to be of importance to the well-being of English departments and their students.

1. Is your department large enough to meet the responsibilities assigned to it by your college or university? Can you serve nonmajors properly and still staff an adequate program for the major in English?

2. Is the distribution of members by rank in your department severely imbalanced? If so, is the imbalance a symptom of stagnation?

3. Has your department surrendered authority in matters crucial

to its welfare? Does it, for example, permit the administration to dictate educational policy?

4. Does your staff include too many specialists, not enough teachers of general ability?

5. Does your department subscribe to and act in accordance with the five guidelines established by the MLA's Commission on the Status of Women in the Profession? (See *PMLA,* 1972, *87*(3).)

6. Are your department's criteria for promotion and tenure well defined and openly declared?

7. Are nontenured members of your department regularly apprised of where they stand? Are they afforded early and ample opportunities to present their cases for promotion and tenure?

8. Do you have a well-considered and clearly enunciated policy on publication?

9. Does your department employ as many methods as possible for evaluating teaching? Does it collect a variety of evidence when teaching competence is to be judged? Does it allow quantifiable evidence (for example, student ratings) to outweigh evidence of other kinds?

10. Are your procedures for sampling students' opinions valid?

11. Is your department's procedure for selecting a new chairman fully democratic?

12. Is the chairman's performance in office regularly and systematically reviewed by those who appoint him? Are department members' opinions of his performance solicited by a confidential procedure?

13. Should your department appoint an assistant chairman to relieve the chairman of easily delegated duties?

14. Does your department hold frequent short meetings, or does it postpone its business until too much has accumulated to be handled properly?

15. Are the duties and provinces of your committees well defined?

16. Are the junior members of your department represented on

your executive committee and your committee on promotion and tenure?

17. Does your department heed its committees, or are the recommendations they have labored to produce frequently ignored or rejected?

18. Are certain courses in your department's curriculum preempted by senior members, or are all courses rotated among those who wish to teach them and are qualified to do so?

19. Do your procedures for achieving uniformity in sectioned courses inhibit individual instructors? For example, does the need to prepare students for common examinations prevent members of your staff from teaching as well as they might?

20. Are reduced teaching loads awarded equitably in your department?

21. Is your department well informed about the teaching loads of other departments at your college or university?

22. Does your department retain adjunct programs (for example, courses in technical writing) that ought to be transferred to other departments?

23. Do all the members of your department teach freshmen? If not, are the exceptions justified?

24. If you offer remedial English, is your program worth the cost?

25. Has your department recently reviewed its policy on exemptions from freshman English? Does your present policy acknowledge the actual abilities of today's students? Should more students be exempted?

26. Does your department offer special counseling to advanced placement students and make every effort to place them in appropriate courses?

27. Does your freshman English program duplicate work many students have done in high school? Are your freshman courses sufficiently rewarding to compete with, say, freshman chemistry or

freshman history? Do your freshman courses afford plenty of opportunities for young teachers to teach with enthusiasm?

28. Has your department recently investigated possibilities of collaborating with other departments to create new interdisciplinary courses or courses in comparative literature?

29. Does your department maintain reciprocal communication with the secondary schools in your community? Are the members of your department well informed about recent developments in secondary education?

30. If your department has a program for training teachers, are its standards for admission high enough to exclude mediocre or incompetent candidates? Would you want your freshmen to be taught in high school by the candidates you admit?

31. Does your teacher-training program meet the guidelines established in 1967 by the English Teacher Preparation Study? (See *PMLA,* 1967, *82*(4).)

32. Does your department offer a sufficient number of courses suitable for sophomores?

33. Are those courses in your curriculum in which most nonmajors enroll designed to encourage continuing delight in literature, or are they designed merely to familiarize students with facts *about* literature?

34. Has your department allowed its curriculum to proliferate by adding too many pet courses which have become the property of individual members?

35. Are most of your classes small enough to permit full discussion of the materials studied?

36. Are the writing assignments in your courses conceived not simply as devices for testing acquired knowledge but also—and primarily—as occasions for students to explore and articulate their developing perceptions?

37. Does your department provide for early majoring? Does it offer special counseling for early majors?

38. Does the major in English continue to attract its share of the best students on your campus? If not, are obsolete requirements discouraging good students from majoring in English? Has your department considered abolishing strict requirements, offering instead several model plans of study, any one of which majors may elect?

39. Does your curriculum include a seed-bed, or courses (for example, freshman seminars, special studies, honors courses) that provide opportunities for experimentation and innovation?

And, finally, one whopping question:

40. Does your department actively resist those who would reduce liberal education to a commercial transaction, and does it continue to assert—by its teaching, the conduct of its affairs, and its presence outside the department—an abiding faith in humane values?

Selected
Bibliography

BAILEY, D. "Faculty Teaching Loads: The State University." *Bulletin of Association of Departments of English,* February 1968, 9–13.

BOOTH, W. "The Undergraduate Program." In J. C. Gerber and others (Eds.), *The College Teaching of English* (New York: Appleton-Century-Crofts, 1965).

BRADDOCK, R., AND ASSOCIATES. *Research in Written Composition.* Champaign, Illinois: National Council of Teachers of English, 1963.

CARTTER, A. M. "Future Faculty: Needs and Resources" In C.B.T. Lee (Ed.), *Improving College Teaching.* Washington, D.C.: American Council on Education, 1967.

COLES, W., JR. "The Teaching of Writing as Writing." *College English,* November 1967, *29,* 111–116.

College Advanced Placement Policies, 1968. Princeton: College Entrance Examination Board, 1968.

CONANT, J. *The Education of American Teachers.* New York: McGraw-Hill, 1963.

CORBETT, E. P. J. "What Is Being Revived?" *College Composition and Communication,* 1967, *18,* 166–172.

DE MOTT, B. "Last Try." In *Voice Project: An Experiment in Teaching Writing to College Freshmen.* Washington, D.C.: Office of Education, 1967.

———. "Reading, Writing, Reality, Unreality . . ." In *Super-grow: Essays and Reports on Imagination in America.* New York: Dutton, 1969.

DIEKHOFF, J. S. *NDEA and Modern Foreign Languages.* New York: MLA, 1965.

DRESSEL, P. L., AND DELISLE, F. H. *Undergraduate Curriculum Trends.* Washington, D.C.: American Council on Education, 1969.

EBLE, K. E. *The Recognition and Evaluation of Teaching.* Project to Improve College Teaching. Washington, D.C.: American Association of University Professors and Association of American Colleges, 1970.

———. *Professors as Teachers.* San Francisco: Jossey-Bass, 1972.

FINCH, J. S. "College English Departments and Teacher Preparation." *PMLA,* 1965, *80,* 3–7.

General Education in a Free Society. Cambridge: Harvard University Press, 1958.

GERBER, J. C. "Literature—Our Untamable Discipline." *College English,* February 1967, *28,* 351–358.

GERBER, J. C., AND OTHERS (Eds.) *The College Teaching of English.* New York: Appleton-Century-Crofts, 1965.

GORRELL, R. "Very Like a Whale—A Report on Rhetoric." *College Composition and Communication,* October 1965, *16,* 138–143.

A Guide to the Advanced Placement Program, 1968-69. New York: College Entrance Examination Board, 1968.

"Guidelines for the Preparation of Teachers of English." *PMLA,* September 1967, *82,* 19–25.

GUSTAD, J. W. "Evaluation of Teaching Performance: Issues and Possibilities." In C.B.T. Lee (Ed.), *Improving College Teaching,* Washington, D.C.: American Council on Education, 1967.

HAMILTON, H. W. "Current Trends in the English Major." *College English,* March 1954, *15,* 339–346.

HARPER, G. M. " 'The Waste Sad Time': Some Remarks on Class Visitation." *College English,* November 1965, *25,* 119–123.

HUDSON, R. H. "The Graduate Record Examination: A Minority Statement and a Prediction." *Bulletin of Association of Departments of English,* 1969, *20,* 50–52.

KENT, L. "Student Evaluation of Teaching." In C.B.T. Lee (Ed.), *Improving College Teaching*. Washington, D.C.: American Council on Education, 1967.

KITZHABER, A. R. *Themes, Theories, and Therapy: The Teaching of Writing in College*. New York: McGraw-Hill, 1963.

LEE, C. B. T. (Ed.) *Improving College Teaching*. Washington, D.C.: American Council on Education, 1967.

MC NAMEE, L. *Ninety-Nine Years of English Dissertations*. Commerce, Texas: East Texas State University, 1969.

MACRORIE, K. *Uptaught*. New York: Hayden, 1970.

MANDEL, B. J. *Literature and the English Department*. Champaign, Ill.: National Council of Teachers of English, 1970.

MARTIN, H. "A College President Speaks Out." *Bulletin of Association of Departments of English*, 1967, *15*, 18–22.

MILIC, L. "Theories of Style and Their Implications for the Teaching of Composition." *College Composition and Communication*, 1965, *16*, 66–69.

MULLER, H. J. *The Uses of English*. New York: Holt, 1967.

National Council of Teachers of English. "The Workload of a College English Teacher: A Proposed Statement of Policy." *College English*, October 1966, *28*, 55–57.

ONG, W. *The Barbarian Within*. New York: Macmillan, 1962.

Open Doors: 1968. Washington, D.C.: Institute of International Education, 1968.

PARKER, W. R. "Where Do English Departments Come From?" *College English*, February 1967, *28*, 339–351.

POLLOCK, T. C. "Should the English Major Be a Cafeteria?" *College English*, March 1954, *15*, 327–331.

POPE, E. M. "Seminars for Freshmen: Report on an Experiment." *Mills College Magazine*, Autumn 1964, 4–10.

RANDEL, W. "English as a Discipline." *College English*, May 1958, *19*, 359–361.

RICE, W. "A Proposal for the Abolition of Freshman English, as It Is Now Commonly Taught, from the College Curriculum." *College English*, April 1960, *21*, 361–367.

ROBERTS, P. "Linguistics and the Teaching of Composition." *English Journal*, May 1963, *52*, 331–335.

ROOSE, K. "How to Be a Department Chairman and Like It." *Bulletin of Association of Departments of English*, September 1969, 35–39.

ROSE, E. S. "English 11–12: Reading and Writing on Human Values:

The What and Why of Freshman English at Haverford College." *Haverford Horizons,* Spring 1964, *5,* 5–6.

ROTHWELL, C. E., AND ASSOCIATES. *The Importance of Teaching: A
Memorandum to the New College Teacher.* Washington, D.C.:
Hazen Foundation, 1968.

SHARPLESS, F. P. "Reflections on *The College Teaching of English."
College English,* October 1967, *29,* 32–39.

SHUGRUE, M. F. *English in a Decade of Change.* New York: Pegasus,
1968.

———. *The National Study of English in the Junior College.* New
York: Modern Language Association, 1969.

SQUIRE, J. R. (Ed.) *A Common Purpose: The Teaching of English
in Great Britain, Canada, and the United States.* Champaign,
Ill.: National Council of Teachers of English, 1966.

———. (Chairman) *The National Interest and the Teaching of
English.* Champaign, Ill.: National Council of Teachers of
English, 1961.

———. "The Running Water and the Standing Stone." *PMLA,*
June 1968, *83,* 523–529.

TATE, G., AND CORBETT, E. P. J. (Eds.) *Teaching Freshman Composition.* New York: Oxford, 1967.

THOMPSON, D. "Aims and Purposes of Teaching English in Britain."
In J. R. Squire (Ed.), *A Common Purpose: The Teaching of
English in Great Britain, Canada, and the United States.*
Champaign, Ill.: National Council of Teachers of English,
1966.

TROWBRIDGE, H. "Introductory Literature Courses." In J. C. Gerber
and others (Eds.), *The College Teaching of English* (New
York: Appleton-Century-Crofts, 1965).

TUTTLE, D. R., AND O'LEARY, H. *Curriculum Patterns in English.*
Washington, D.C.: U.S. Government Printing Office, 1965.

UTLEY, F. L. "The Boundaries of Language and Rhetoric: The English
Curriculum." *College Composition and Communication,* May
1968, *19,* 125–130.

WERDELL, P. *Course and Teacher Evaluation: A Student's Confidential
Guide.* Washington, D.C.: United States National Student
Association, 1966.

WOLF, M. H. *Effect of Writing Frequency upon Proficiency in a College
Freshman English Course.* Cooperative Research Program of
the Office of Education, Project No. 2846. Amherst: University
of Massachusetts, 1966,

Index